FADEN'S MAP OF NORFOLK

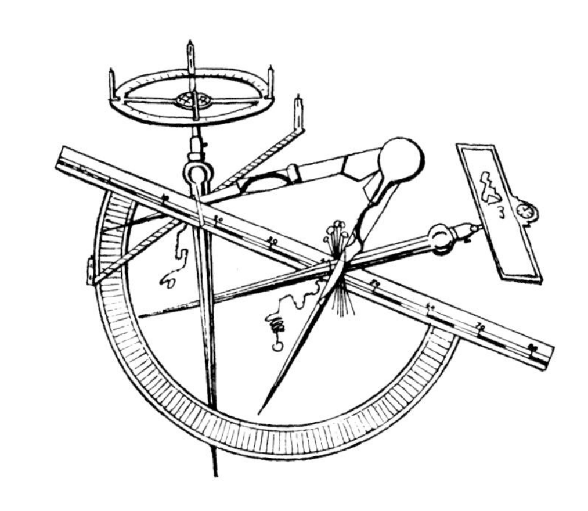

Introduction by J. C. Barringer

Small maps drawn by David Yaxley

Larks Press Edition

Published by
The Larks Press
Ordnance Farmhouse, Guist Bottom, Dereham, Norfolk NR20 5PF
Fax/Tel 01328 829207
Printed and bound at the Witley Press Ltd., Hunstanton

First printed May 1989
Reprinted 1992, 1996, 1998, 2001, 2004

ACKNOWLEDGEMENTS
We are grateful to the Norfolk Record Society for permission to use their printing of Faden's map in the production of this edition. We also wish to thank Chris Barringer for permission to reprint his introduction to the map and for his helpful advice and encouragement.

ISBN 0 948400 09 9

An Introduction to Faden's Map of Norfolk

by J. C. Barringer, M.A.

This introduction was first published by the Norfolk Record Society with the six-sheet edition of Faden's map in 1975. It is published here by kind permission of the Society and the author, J. C. Barringer. The footnotes and appendices have been omitted from this edition, but may be found in the Norfolk Record Society Volume XLII.

1. Faden and his map.

William Faden, geographer to King George III and the Prince of Wales, published his map of Norfolk on 12 August 1797. In the heading to the map he described himself as being its proprietor and publisher. The actual surveying for the map was carried out for Faden by Thomas Donald, Thomas Milne and assistants. Perhaps because he was owner of the map it has become known as Faden's map. This is in contrast to the nearly contemporary map of Suffolk which is known by the name of its surveyor, Hodskinson, though Faden engraved and published it. It seems that Faden's financial control of the Norfolk map entitled him to consider it as his map and to submit it for an award from the Royal Society of Arts.

In 1759 this society had begun to encourage the large-scale mapping of the counties of England and Wales. As Harley has pointed out in an interesting series of articles in the *Journal of the Royal Society of Arts*, this encouragement, given by the award of gold medals and premiums, led to a number of surveys being submitted. Joseph Hodskinson proffered his map of Suffolk and gained a gold medal in 1784. It was however Faden who applied to the Society for the Norfolk map to be considered for an award, having already received awards for his maps of Hampshire and Sussex in 1793 and 1795 respectively. He wrote to the secretary of the Society of Arts on 4 April 1798 from his address at Charing Cross: 'I have herewith taken the liberty of troubling you with a new topographical map of the County of Norfolk, surveyed in the years 1790, 91, 92, 93 and 94 and planned by a scale of one inch to a statute mile - it is the only map of the above county extant which has been constructed from actual measurements. I request, sir, you will have the kindness to lay it before the Committee of the Society for the Encouragement of Arts, Manufacturers and Commerce for their examination and patronage. With respect to the character of the map I beg leave to refer the gentlemen of the committee to the two accompanying letters received from opposite parts of the County......' The two gentlemen referred to were Thomas William Coke of Holkham and Joseph Windham of Earsham House near Bungay. In a letter dated 23 October 1797, Joseph Windham declared the map to be 'the best executed survey he has seen, and has no doubt Mr. Faden will receive the credit for it he is justly entitled to ......In one sheet (near Attleborough) there is a place called Caston which is spelled Coston in these places, the sheets not yet delivered might be corrected with a pen...Mr. W. desires you have his 2nd copy laid by till he sees Mr. Faden'. Coke's letter was also complimentary.

Faden's application was discussed by the Committee of Polite Arts on 7 April 1798. True to the style of the best committees it was 'resolved that the further consideration of the map be postponed and in the meantime that the secretary write to Mr. Faden to communicate to the committee the information by which he claims any and to what degree of superiority in the map; and that he also be requested to obtain any such information from the gentleman who has surveyed the County of Norfolk under the direction of the House of Commons, and also from the Post Master General as may supply the committee with corroborating evidence in favour of the improvement of this map'. The committee met again on 2 May 1798 and concluded 'that the survey is very accurate but not having been begun as proposed in the advertisement it cannot be considered as a claim of the premium offered'.

The 'advertisement' was that in which the society had announced the conditions under which awards would be made. These conditions included a stipulation that maps should be completed within one or at most two years. It was apparently this clause which prevented Faden qualifying for an award since his map had been surveyed over a period of five years. The Society decided to buy one copy of the map for its records, but William Faden received neither gold medal nor premium for his Norfolk map.

Faden also published many other maps during his career: a catalogue listing his works published in 1822 included 350 items. His office in Charing Cross was an important centre for all matters cartographical, as was recognised by his position of 'Geographer to the King and to the Prince of Wales'.

In 1801 he published the first county survey (Kent) to be 'done by the surveying draughtsmen of His Majesty's Honourable Board of Ordnance, on the basis of the Trigonometrical Survey'. The Ordnance Board's next map, that of Essex, issued in 1805, was however both engraved and published at the Tower. Faden obviously had very close links with the surveyors and engravers who were employed by the Board of Ordnance. One of the few references to the surveyors who worked on his Norfolk map reveals Thomas Milne applying unsuccessfully for a post with the Board of Ordnance.

The suggestion made to Faden by the Polite Arts Committee of the Society of Arts that he should contact 'the gentleman who has surveyed the county of Norfolk under the direction of the House of Commons', raises the question as to whether Faden had a part-completed survey already available which he was able to complete. Limited research has not revealed the identity of the 'gentleman' nor the government department for which he was making his survey. It is clear however that the Society of Arts was aware of some surveying activity already taking place in Norfolk. Harley has noted the existence of a War Office map of Norfolk in the Public Record Office. This has been examined; it is a map of part of the County 'from Lynn Regis to Yarmouth, including Norwich', drawn in 1793 at exactly one inch to one statute mile; its extent is shown in Figure I. It is incomplete, the River Wensum between Fakenham and Norwich being shown only in pencil and all relief being in light pencil hachures. All the greens and commons are clearly shown but many other details had obviously not been plotted when work on it ceased. The Norfolk pronunciation clearly proved too much for the surveyor of the Aylsham area who had noted 'Buargh next Aylsham, Slowley, Swynton Abbots, Skyton, Bramton, Oxned and Scottaw. Marshes were mapped in green and the detail of the coast and coastal settlements was shown very fully. It is not possible to say whether this unfinished map is the work of the 'Gentleman..... under the direction of the House of Commons' or whether it is an early draft of part of Faden's map on which the field surveyors' unamended interpretations of place-names had been recorded. If it

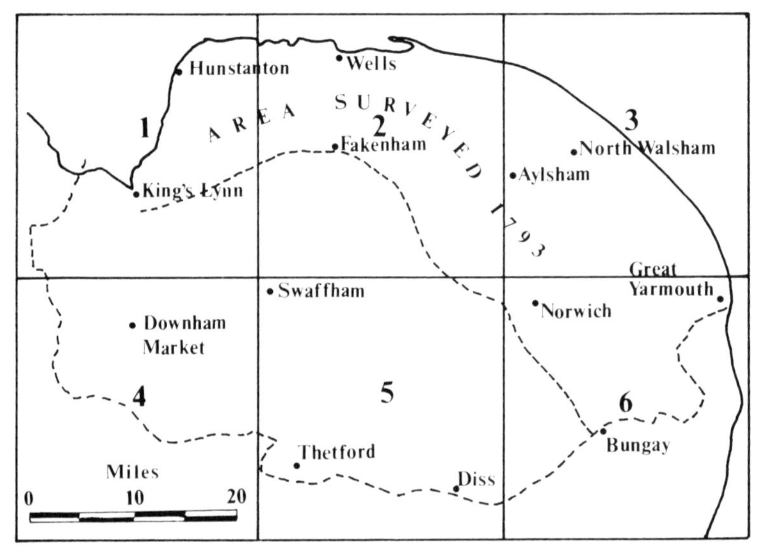

Figure I. The six sheets of Faden's map

is the latter there is no obvious reason why work on it should have ceased.

Another possibility is that the Board of Ordnance surveyors were at work in Norfolk when Faden began his survey in 1790. It is clear from William Mudge's *Account of the Operations carried on for accomplishing a Trigonometrical Survey of England and Wales* that no work had been carried out in Norfolk down to 1790. Mudge's three volumes give full details of the progress of the triangulation of Great Britain and in Volume III, Plate I there is a full plan of the principal triangles of England, Wales and part of Scotland. Two Norfolk sites, Lynn Old Tower and Downham Spire are the only Norfolk stations shown on that plan. Suffolk was only tied into the survey in 1799 and then the most northerly stations were at Lavenham, Naughton, Henby, Otley, Woodbridge, Butley and Orford lighthouse. Even as late as 1809 Norfolk and parts of Lincolnshire remained outside the system of principal triangles. In view of this evidence it seems that no official army triangulation had been carried out in Norfolk by the time that Faden's map was published.

It is interesting that this map, in contrast to the eighteenth-century maps of Lancashire and Suffolk has no diagram showing the system of triangulation used by its surveyors. This means that it is not known where the base line measurements were made nor which were the key stations for the triangulation. Such an omission might seem to suggest that Faden did not actually carry out the basic triangulation and could not justifiably include the appropriate diagrams; but with the apparent absence of any other surveyors at work in the county it must be assumed that Faden's team was responsible for this triangulation.

The techniques of surveying were improving steadily during the eighteenth century. It is almost certain that angular measurements were made with a theodolite and that the detail was mapped in on a plane table with measurements being made by a gunters chain of 66 feet in length (4 poles at 5½ yards to the pole). The early surveying books, for example Hammond's *Practical Surveyor* (1731), give full details of both theodolite and plane table surveying methods. Such developments allowed increasingly accurate maps to be made in the eighteenth century, no doubt partly in response to demand from enclosing landlords for accurate parish and estate maps. A map was tied in to its position on the surface of the globe by precise determination of latitude and longitude: again the invention of the accurate chronometer by John Harrison in 1772 allowed east-west dimensions of large areas to be much more accurately plotted than previously.

In summary it does seem likely, in view of the time spent in making the map and in view of the other evidence mentioned, that Faden's team of surveyors was responsible for all or nearly all of both the triangulation and mapping of local detail on this first large-scale map of Norfolk.

2. Description of the map.

Faden advertised his new map in the following terms in the *Norfolk Chronicle* of 19 August, 1797:

'A New Topographical Map of the
COUNTY OF NORFOLK
surveyed and measured in the years 1790, 91, 92, 93 and 94.
By Tho. Donald, Tho. Milne
AND ASSISTANTS.
Planned from a scale of one inch to a statute mile.
Executed and published at the expense of the proprietor,
William Faden, Geographer to his Majesty, and to H.R.H.
the Prince of Wales.

In the above map are described all the seats of the nobility and gentry, woods, parks, heaths, commons, rivers, great and cross roads, marsh and fen lands, market towns, parishes, villages, farms etc. Also the remains of Roman roads, camps and other antiquities; embellished with plans of the towns of Great Yarmouth, Lynn and Swaffham. The map is printed on six sheets of the largest atlas paper. Price to subscribers is Two Guineas and a half, in sheets; to non-subscribers it will be three guineas.

Subscriptions are received in the county by Roger Kerrison and Bartlett Gurney Esq., at their several Banks and by the proprietor of the map, W. Faden, Charing Cross, London. The subscription will close on the 31st day of December next, when a list of subscribers will be printed.

Note subscribers' maps will be ready for delivery on the 1st day of October next; and to non-subscribers on the 1st day of January 1798. Charing Cross August 5 1797.'

Faden issued the map in six sheets as shown in figure I ; the only known copy in six sheets is in the British Museum. Normally the sheets have been segmented and mounted on linen as in the copy belonging to the Norwich Colman Rye Library which has been used for this edition. The full dimensions of the map are 66½ inches east to west by 48 inches north to south.

The surveyors plotted their map to a scale of one inch to one statute mile and the plates were engraved exactly to this scale, but the paper apparently contracted slightly during printing so that the published map is to a scale of 1 inch to 1 mile 36 yards 2 feet. Longitude is expressed on two scales; one giving minutes and seconds of time, the other showing degrees of longitude east of the Greenwich meridian. We thus find that 15 minutes of arc of longitude equals one minute of time. The east and west margins show degrees and minutes of latitude. The spherical nature of the earth means that degrees of longitude decrease with latitude, there is therefore a problem of representing this shape on a flat paper surface. Faden apparently used a simple form of projection and has a central meridian to his map rather than using the Greenwich meridian; this technique was followed by the Ordnance Survey in their first edition of the six inch to one mile county maps. In practice it means that a Norfolk map could not be matched up with a Cambridge map to its west. Faden gives astronomical observations to fix Great Yarmouth and King's Lynn, it is from these that he would tie in his survey unless he relied on other determined points also. These observations appear to have been fairly accurately determined; St. Nicholas' Chapel Lynn is shown 54 seconds south of its true latitude and 1 minute too far west, and Great Yarmouth church is given 40 seconds south of its correct latitude and 1 minute 38 seconds too far west.

Conventional Signs

The conventional signs used were shown in a key, or 'explanation' in the south-west sheet. This key did not indicate that Hundreds were distinguished by the largest capital letters used, and their boundaries defined by a fine dotted line. Hundred boundaries are important in many aspects of historical research and although earlier maps showed them, they are more accurately depicted on Faden's map.

Parish boundaries were not shown by Faden and it was Bryant's map of Norfolk, produced in 1826 at a scale of 1. 22 inches to a mile which first showed both parish and Hundred boundaries. The first edition of the Ordnance Survey's Norfolk map (1838) showed the parish boundaries but not those of the Hundreds.

Relief was shown on Faden's map by a system of hachures. This was the first attempt to give an overall impression of relief in the county as opposed to showing 'mountains'. Robert Morden, for example, showed isolated jagged peaks in north Norfolk. Whilst Faden's hachures gave a much more effective impression of relief than Morden's system, they still created an impression of exaggerated relief, Poringland Heath for example appearing as a high plateau. The engraving used by the Ordnance Survey in their first edition was finer than that used by Faden and enabled a subtler degree of relief to be shown. Before using either map for detailed field work it is worth making a comparative study of the two surveys in order to see which achieves the better representation of the relief of any particular area of the county.

Faden's spelling of some place-names varied interestingly from that used today. The inhabitants of Silfield will note with some disquiet that Faden recorded their hamlet as Sinfield. Themelthorpe was noted as Thembelthorpe, as it still is known locally, and many more small variations, probably related to dialect pronunciations, are to be noted.

3. Evaluation of the map.

Until the 1790s the largest scale map of Norfolk was that surveyed by James Corbridge in 1730 at a scale of two miles to one inch. This 'Survey of the County of Norfolk...' emphasized the main roads of the county but was crude in its detailing (see for example the north Norfolk coast). Other detail shown, such as a large continuous broad between Martham and Waxham, raises interesting questions as to the extent of physical changes between the 1730s and the 1790s. Corbridge also, like Faden, gave the names of the occupiers of the main houses in Norfolk, or perhaps more correctly, of those who had subscribed to his map.

Norfolk has been divided by many writers into a number of distinctive regions. In assessing the value of the map as a geographical and historical record the main regions will be discussed first; and then its portrayal of the settlement pattern of the county and of past agricultural systems will be examined. The question of the accuracy of the map is interwoven with that of its value as a record of natural and human change. It is doubtful, for example, if we can trust Faden's surveyors' measurements sufficiently to be able to assess the rate of erosion of the cliffs of Overstrand since 1797; on the other hand the representation of a windmill or a brick-kiln almost certainly means that one existed very near to the position indicated. 'Very near' is not near enough to be a basis for exact measurement, but it is sufficiently accurate to enable us to start looking on the ground for the physical remains of a windmill or a brick-kiln.

Regional Evaluation

I. The Coast

The outline of the south coast of the Wash has changed completely since 1797. Faden helpfully dated to 1791 the outermost sea bank immediately north of Walpole Cross Keys and to 1774 that to the north of what is now Admiral's Farm. Two and a half miles of marshes have since been reclaimed outside the 1791 wall. Faden's dating of the progression of the embanking shows that reclamation was proceeding fast in the late eighteenth century. Sutton Bridge, now a considerable settlement, was then a scatter of houses together with the Cross Keys House from which a two-mile route lay at low water across the marshes to Walpole Cross Keys. The Nene outfall has been extended five miles seawards from Gunthorpe sluice since 1797. Further east the estuary of the Great Ouse has also changed since Faden's day. The outstanding difference is the realignment of the outfall of the river so that North Lynn, shown by Faden to the west of the river, has gone and the river channel has been brought well to the west of its position in 1797 thus allowing marshes to be reclaimed between the east wall of the channel and North and South Wootton. Further east still the coastline at Wells has also changed. The site in front of the town, now covered by tents and caravans during the summer, was an area of tidal water in the 1790s, the long sea wall not being built until 1859. Blakeney Point has continued its westerly growth since the 1790s and the entrance to Blakeney harbour is now even more tortuous than it was then.

As already mentioned the small scale of the map makes it difficult to assess how much land has been lost to the sea. Even so, much can be learnt. Cromer lighthouse, built in 1719, is shown by Faden to be near the cliff edge; by 1832 it was so threatened that a second light was built and that shown by Faden went into the sea in 1866. The map thus has great value in helping us to establish another fixed point in a sequence of change. Sidestrand church was shown at the head of an area of 'beech' in 1797 but some way from the sea; whatever the degree of accuracy of the location this building had to be replaced in 1880.

Faden noted the change in the nature of the coast south of Happisburgh from mud cliffs to the 'Marum Hills' and he also carefully recorded nine breaches in the Marum Hills which had occurred up to the summer of 1792; this reminds us that the great floods of 1938 and 1953 were by no means the first on this stretch of coast. The navigational problems faced by shipping in rounding Winterton Ness were reflected by there being lights on the Ness itself and a further two at Winterton. The long sandspit on which Great Yarmouth evolved has not grown since the 1790s; this is because the Port of Yarmouth; having finally achieved a stable outlet after many earlier breaches of the sand bank, managed to control the position of the outfall of the River Yare. The portrayal of all these coastal features is far more detailed than on any earlier Norfolk map and gives many new facts that are of topographical and historical importance.

II. The Breckland

There are great differences between the late eighteenth-century Breckland and that of today. Mr St. Payne Galway lived at West Tofts and the first of the now familiar shelter-belts had been planted around his estate. A letter written by Galway to Lord Petre of Buckenham Hall in 1788 makes reference to the planting that was then being carried out by Lord Petre and refers also to his own scheme of planting. It is probably true that in the late eighteenth century, Norfolk had less woodland than at any other time in its history. The open heaths of Croxton, Santon and Mundham stretched far and wide. Sturston and Stanford both had warrens. In the Thet and Little Ouse valleys open fields appear to have survived later than in other parts of the county, such fields being noted at Kilverston and Brettenham. It is of course possible that the names outlived the reality of an open-field system of farming, as is suggested by the fact that the first edition of the Ordnance Survey map also notes a number of 'fields' well after enclosure had taken place, for example near Fakenham.

The meres are one of Breckland's most interesting features. Donald and Milne seem to have been selective as to which they named. Ringmere and Langmere for example were not named and their boundaries were shown as being irregular. Were they in fact less regular in shape than now? Two small meres are shown either side of the Peddars Way immediately to the north of the Norwich-Thetford road. They are almost exactly on the line of the railway and presumably were drained and filled in when it was built in 1846. Further north on the Peddars Way, Thompson Water had not yet been made, a sheep-wash being the only recorded feature on that stretch of the small Thompson tributary of the River Wissey. Nineteenth-century enclosures together with the later activities of the Forestry Commission have greatly altered the nature of the region of heath, warrens and meres since it was recorded by the late eighteenth-century surveyors.

III. The Broads

Figure II gives a sample of the detail shown by Faden for the area of the

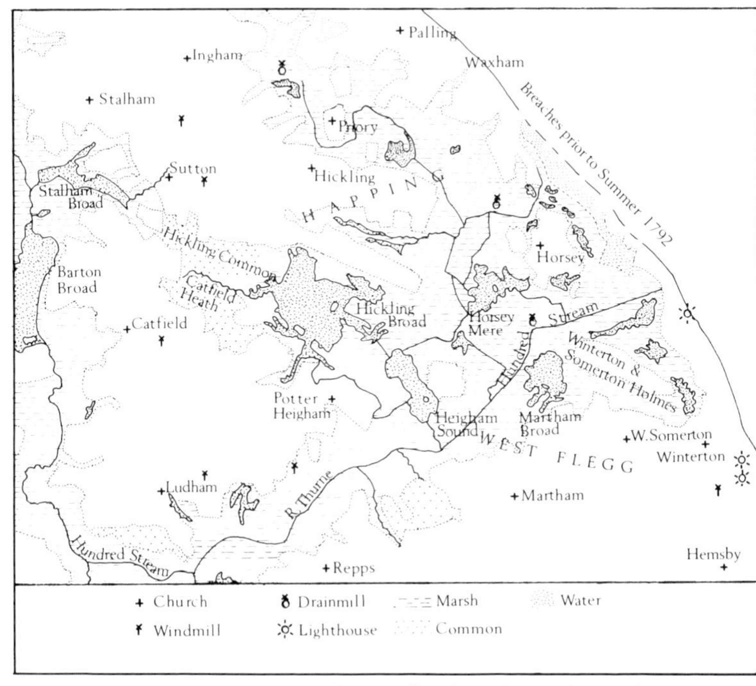

Figure II. A part of Broadland as shown by Faden

Norfolk Broads. The changes in this area are striking. As with the Breckland meres there is some doubt as to how accurately areas of water have been delineated. Detail apart, however, the recording of broads which have subsequently disappeared is probably accurate. A manuscript map of Hickling in 1810 clearly shows three broads — Wigg's, Gage's and Hare Park — to the north of Hickling Broad. On this evidence it would seem that Faden's reading of these features was relatively reliable. The information as to the existence of drainage mills (for example that marked at Waxham in 1797) is also valuable. Staithes too were shown. Hickling's Staithe House was marked, but Ludham Staithe, laid out at the time of the Ludham Enclosure Award in 1800, together with the new cut up Womack Water, had not then been constructed. Many more details, such as the position of Ludham's windmill or of Stalham Wood by Wayford Bridge, also help to give a valuable picture of Broadland nearly two hundred years ago.

IV. The Fens

The geography of the Fenland has altered more since 1797 than that of any other part of the county. The major changes of the coast have already been noted. Inland, although the two major drainage lines of the Old and New Bedford Levels were cut in 1636 and 1652 respectively, many areas of badly drained fen remained. Marshland Fen was not drained until the major addition of the Middle Level Main Drain from Three Holes to Wiggenhall St. Mary was cut in 1848. As can be seen from the map, Marshland Fen and Smeeth and Magdalen Fens were still grazing areas in the 1790s and were almost certainly under water for most of the winter. The drier northern silt-fen shows up clearly with its distinctive linear greens at Tilney, Terrington and the Walpoles, all of which were bounded by nearly continuous settlement. After the later drainage the new parish of Marshland St. James was created out of this area of former common grazing-land.

In the south-east corner of the Norfolk Fens, the 'islands' of Hilgay and Southery stood out clearly above their surrounding marshes, and although Sams Cut Drain from Feltwell to Hilgay Bridge had already been excavated by the 1790s the land bordering it was still only suitable for grazing cattle. The whole of this area with its dry common and warren either side of Methwold and the wet grazing-lands on the Fen has changed as much as any in the county since the map was drawn.

V. Central (High) Norfolk

Many of the comments which have already been made apply as well to the central part of the county as do comments on other features which are dealt with in the section which evaluates some of the principal elements of the landscape as shown in 1797. Parts of central Norfolk have changed less than areas which have already been discussed. The maze of small lanes and isolated farms in the area around Dereham or in the zone between Diss and Attleborough is remarkably unchanged as compared with the built-up areas of the coast and the drained fenland. The commons have in the main gone; in some places, such as Tacolneston and Forncett, the common fields were shown as 'lately enclosed' in 1797. Some wood has disappeared, Morningthorpe for example has lost its wood and Hempnall its grove. The structure of villages nearest to Norwich has of course changed the most, but generally speaking change has perhaps been less marked in central Norfolk than in the marginal areas of the Fens, Breckland and Broads.

VI. The Inset Town Plans

Saxton and Speed both gave inset plans of Norwich in their maps of Norfolk of 1574 and 1611 respectively. It is a pity that Faden did not do so and the map of the city that is the most nearly contemporary with his map of the county is that made by Anthony Hochstetter in 1789. Perhaps the slight gain from this omission is that Faden added maps of Great Yarmouth and King's Lynn at scales of approximately fifteen inches and ten inches to the mile respectively and one of Swaffham at approximately thirteen inches to the mile.

Faden's map of Great Yarmouth had been preceded by three others made in 1730, 1753, and 1779 respectively. The 1730 map is on a smaller scale than Faden's and gives no detail of building plans between the rows; the 1779 map has not been examined but that of 1753 - a manuscript map by Swinden - was drawn at the large scale of fifty-three inches to a mile (one inch to one and a half chains). An examination of the detail on Swinden's map suggests that Faden almost certainly used it as a source for his very detailed inset map. The area around the bowling-green on the quay, opposite the modern site of Vauxhall Station, is very similar on Faden's map to that shown by Swinden. The latter's surveying of the infill between the rows gives much information. The area around St. George's Chapel is also shown unchanged between 1753 and 1797. It would seem likely that in view of the existence of a survey at such a large scale, Faden's surveyors would at least have used it as a base map. The main additions added in 1797 seem to be a number of rope-walks on the Denes and four cannon on the Mount in front of St. George's Chapel.

King's Lynn had also been mapped earlier in the eighteenth century. William Rastrick's map of 1725 was drawn at a much larger scale than Faden's and therefore gave more detail; Rastrick was able to show house-plots diagrammatically and to give street-names. Some changes had taken place however between 1725 and 1797. Faden recorded two brick-kilns tucked away in the north-east corner embayments of the defences. Perhaps the most important details shown were those of the proposed line of the Eau Brink Cut and of the new sea-walls which it was hoped would improve the navigation up river to Lynn. The overall impression however is that Lynn had not grown much between 1725 and 1797; indeed an even earlier map, dated 1683 shows that Lynn was virtually as large then as in 1797.

The plan of Swaffham is in some ways the most significant of the three since there is no earlier known map of the town and the tithe-map of 1843 was the next to be made. The charming compact market-place has changed little since 1797 but the Crown Inn which stood at its northern side has gone, as has the theatre at its north-western corner on the Lynn road. The parsonage then lay in the north-western corner of the churchyard, a large pond and town-pit cutting almost completely across the southern end of the market-place. The Camping Land was called the Shooting Land by Faden and the Free School sat firmly in its centre. It is difficult to assess the accuracy of Faden's block plans of buildings, but if they are to be relied upon at all both the manor house and the manor farm group of buildings have changed considerably since the 1790s.

VII. Norwich

As has been said, Faden did not produce his own inset map of Norwich and the detailing of the city is therefore very limited. The present boundary of the County and City of Norwich was already largely established. Many windmills were marked as were two lime-kilns but none of the brick-fields to the west of Queens Road nor those in Sprowston were shown. Eaton was named Easton: this must be an error because it was never named as such in much earlier accounts. The toll-gate shown on the Dereham road is a reminder of the existence of the turnpike system at that time. Earlham Park was clearly shown as were the properties in South Catton owned by a trio of the Harvey family. The features of the city within the walls were shown very diagrammatically and Hochstetter's map must be examined for further detail of the main part of the city as it existed in the 1780s.

Evaluation of Principal Elements of the Landscape

I. The Nature and Distribution of Settlement

(a) In the Past

Faden's advertisement stressed that his map showed 'the remains of Roman roads, camps and other antiquities'. The map is inconsistent in its recording of antiquities. Burial mounds, for example those in the Merton/Tottington and East Harling areas, were not shown whereas Warham Camp was marked. Wymondham Abbey was only recorded as a parish church. Other sites which we now take for granted such as Elmham Cathedral and

Caistor by Yarmouth had not then been recognised as having archaeological significance. The roads leading to Norwich from Kenninghall, Scole and Bungay were named Ikenield Street, Pye Street and Stone Street respectively by Faden. It is interesting to speculate on the evidence that he may have used for marking these roads as antiquities.

(b) Domestic Buildings and Churches

How far we can rely on Faden to have included all substantial structures is an important question in assessing the value of the map as a reliable document. An example of an omission is that of Gonville Hall and its associated buildings just to the west of Wymondham. White Rail Farm, another early farm with outbuildings which overlooked Great Melton Common is also omitted. In the same area there are many more buildings shown on the north side of the main road at the west end of Hethersett than appear on a contemporaneous map of 1799.

One or two aspects of the settlement shown on the map are particularly interesting. In the case of Whitwell, just to the west of Reepham, Faden noted 'Demolished' under the name of the parish: the same note is written in under Kerdiston as well. The modern Ordnance Survey map notes the site of a chapel in Kerdiston and the moated site of Giants Hall: Faden clearly had some evidence on which to imply a former chapel site or, more problematically, a village site. In the case of Whitwell the problem is more difficult. Yet fieldwork and excavation have revealed that there are the remains of buildings in the meadows to the east of Whitwell Hall: it seems therefore that Faden's note was based on some buildings surviving there in 1797 or on a report that they had existed. In the same area he shows only one church instead of the two that actually stood in Reepham churchyard so that his reliability must again be questioned: when however a church is marked as being in ruins the information is almost certainly reliable.

(c) Public Buildings and Industrial Sites

The map shows wind and water-mills, drainage-mills and brick-kilns. If the valley of the River Bure is examined on the map many interesting industrial details are revealed; for example at Horstead a water-mill, a lime-kiln and a marl-pit are marked and at Coltishall a brew-office. The limits of scale prevented this sort of detail being shown in the larger settlements because of the problem of obscuring the delineation of buildings, but details of local industry could be given at smaller sites. The map shows a smithy at Plumstead, near Baconsthorpe; a 'Tan-Office' is marked west of Holt and the workhouse to its east; yet at Whitwell, already referred to, a tannery site with a mill-pond is not specified, nor is Reepham brewery nor any of its brick-kilns. At Lyng on the other hand the paper-mill was specified. As with other aspects of the settlement pattern it would seem that the specification of industrial activities is not consistent.

In summary it can be said that when Faden showed a named farm, a house belonging to a specified individual, a mill or a kiln it can be assumed to have existed. As far as other unspecified buildings were concerned it almost certainly meant that a diagrammatic representation of settlement was used; in addition it has been shown that some buildings were omitted.

II. Commons and Greens

Faden published his map when parliamentary enclosure was gaining momentum. Many of the commons and greens he showed were to disappear within a decade, while by the time Bryant's map was published in 1826 nearly all had gone. This gives a particular interest to the distribution of commons as shown by Faden.

The mapping of commons, heaths, greens and warrens appears to have been accurately done, as is shown by a comparison between the enclosure-award map for Mattishall and Faden's map. This reveals that the boundaries of Mattishall's three commons - Badley Moor, South Green and the Heath -

are accurately represented though the naming of two of the commons as West Green and Hall Green is not supported by contemporary evidence. The commons of Watton, too, were accurately mapped, Faden recording an 'island' of already enclosed land on what he termed Low Common. In a few cases the surveyors may have been able to use pre-enclosure surveys to help them, Kimberley and Carlton Forehoe for example had been mapped in 1766, but most of the Norfolk parishes for which maps survive were not enclosed until the first decade of the nineteenth century, so that it seems that Faden's survey was a precursor of most of these large-scale maps. It is possible that his county-wide record of commons made landowners realise just how much land remained unenclosed by the end of the century.

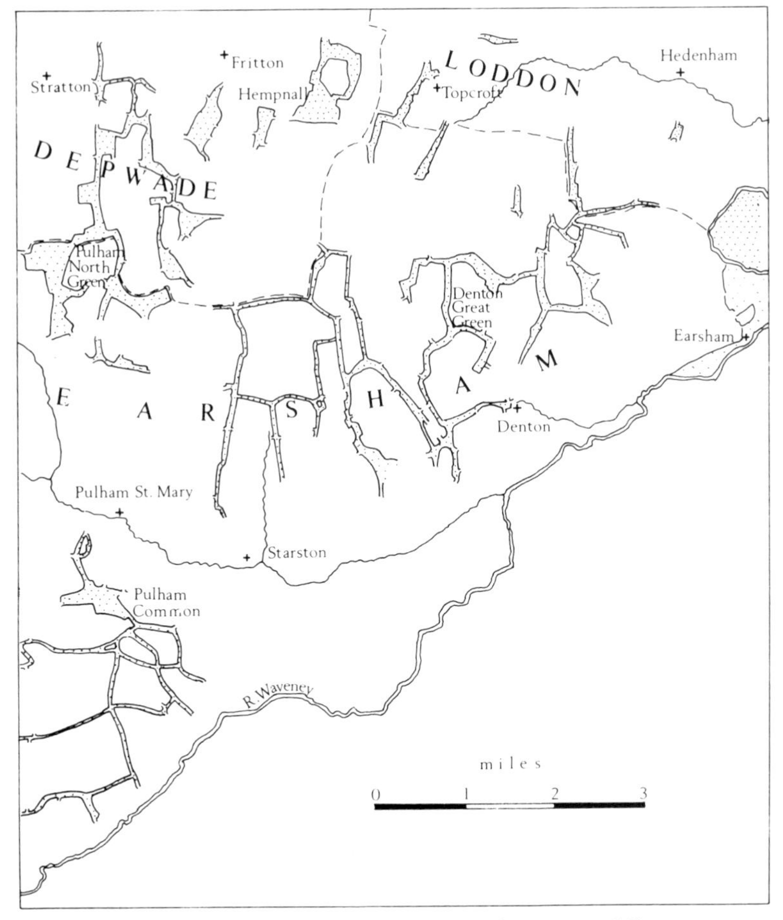

Figure III. Commons and greens in south-east Norfolk, 1797.

Mention had already been made of the great extent of the warrens and heaths in the Breckland. Figure III shows the greens and commons of an area in south-east Norfolk as recorded by Faden. It reveals a pattern of linear commons and greens some of which were virtually 'street' greens. These reflect the pastoral economy of this part of Norfolk, with its need for drove-roads for long distance movement of stock to market and more locally between the commons and the villages. Of the greens and commons shown, that at Fritton has survived to remind us what a medieval common looked like, though in all probability the pasture, because of grazing and manuring, would have been far better than that which now exists. Faden's map shows very clearly the way in which farms and cottages had been located around the edge of these commons (as at Hempnall), where the owners could take advantage of the grazing for stock and where, as population pressed on land, they might secure a sliver of former common land in order to build a cottage. That the final stage of the long process of the enclosure of common lands was under way is seen in one or two places where Faden notes 'lately enclosed' across former common lands; Winfarthing Common is a good example of this. It is perhaps as a last record of remnants of the medieval system of commons that this map has one of its greatest values.

III. Communications

There is much of interest to be found in the detail of the road system. The main roads from Norwich were shown accurately for the first time on Ogilby's strip maps in his *Britannia* (1675). The suggestion made by the committee of the Society of Arts to Faden that he consult the Post Master General also implies that a great deal of information about roads already existed.

The fine-drawn network of minor roads was shown in more detail by Faden than by any previous cartographer. A close examination of the Besthorpe-Bunwell area south-west of Wymondham shows that many changes have taken place in the minor road system since the end of the eighteenth century. Spooner Row did not exist as a distinct settlement according to Faden and a maze of tracks linked up isolated farms which stood beside the many small commons in the area. During enclosure new, straight, wide-verged roads were laid out such as those now running from the Norwich-Thetford road to Spooner Row station and from Spooner Row to New Buckenham. The recasting of the road system which resulted from the enclosures has meant that many tracks marked by Faden have disappeared, but evidence of their existence in 1797 cannot be used to prove rights of way since these were re-specified in the spate of enclosure acts passed subsequent to the printing of Faden's map.

The pattern of main roads in the county has also changed considerably in the past two hundred years. The new coast-road, the modern A17, was made around the southern edge of the Wash in 1817. In Faden's day Wisbech was the lowest bridging point on the Nene and Wiggenhall St. Germains on the Great Ouse, so that the isolation of the Fenland villages was then far greater than now. It was the wide wet marshlands which imposed the severest control on movement in Norfolk in Faden's day; the marshes from Acle to Yarmouth, for instance, had no road across them until 1820. The Hundred Stream still divided West Flegg from Happing Hundred as it had done for a thousand years. Travellers could follow the high-water mark along the coast from Caistor to Happisburgh but no coast-road existed. In this part of Norfolk, boat was the easiest form of transport. Milestones were recorded throughout the county on the main roads and in north Norfolk direction posts were also indicated near the coast. Surprisingly, the map is not very informative about the turnpike roads of Faden's day. Although nearly all the main roads in the county had been turnpiked during the decade 1760-70, tollgates are noted rather erratically. On the Norwich-Thetford road they are not marked outside Norwich or Thetford but that at Fettlebridge near Attleborough is shown.

The rivers, as has been noted, were of greater value in the 1790s than today. Canals have never been so important in East Anglia as in the more heavily industrialised parts of the country, but some small schemes, really the canalisation of rivers, were carried out. The Bure Navigation was in existence in 1797 and the locks between Coltishall and Aylsham were all shown by Faden. The North Walsham and Dilham Canal and the New Cut from Reedham to Haddiscoe had still to be built, so that the timing of eighteenth-century river navigation can be well assessed by following the waterways as shown on the map. Other interesting features connected with navigation were the staithes, Faden recording one at Cantley on the Yare. Wind provided the power for pumping water and many mill sites were marked which have subsequently disappeared as they have been replaced by diesel engines.

Any commentary on a map of an entire county must be selective especially since the wealth of detail shown on this first one inch survey of the county is vast. The accuracy and reliability of the map appears to have varied with the features shown; scale inevitably imposed its limitations on the degree of detail that could be shown. It is however the first complete large-scale record of Norfolk that we have; and it is the only one produced before the great changes consequent upon enclosure, population migration, the building of the railways, and the impact of the motor car, had imposed their new patterns on the face of the county.

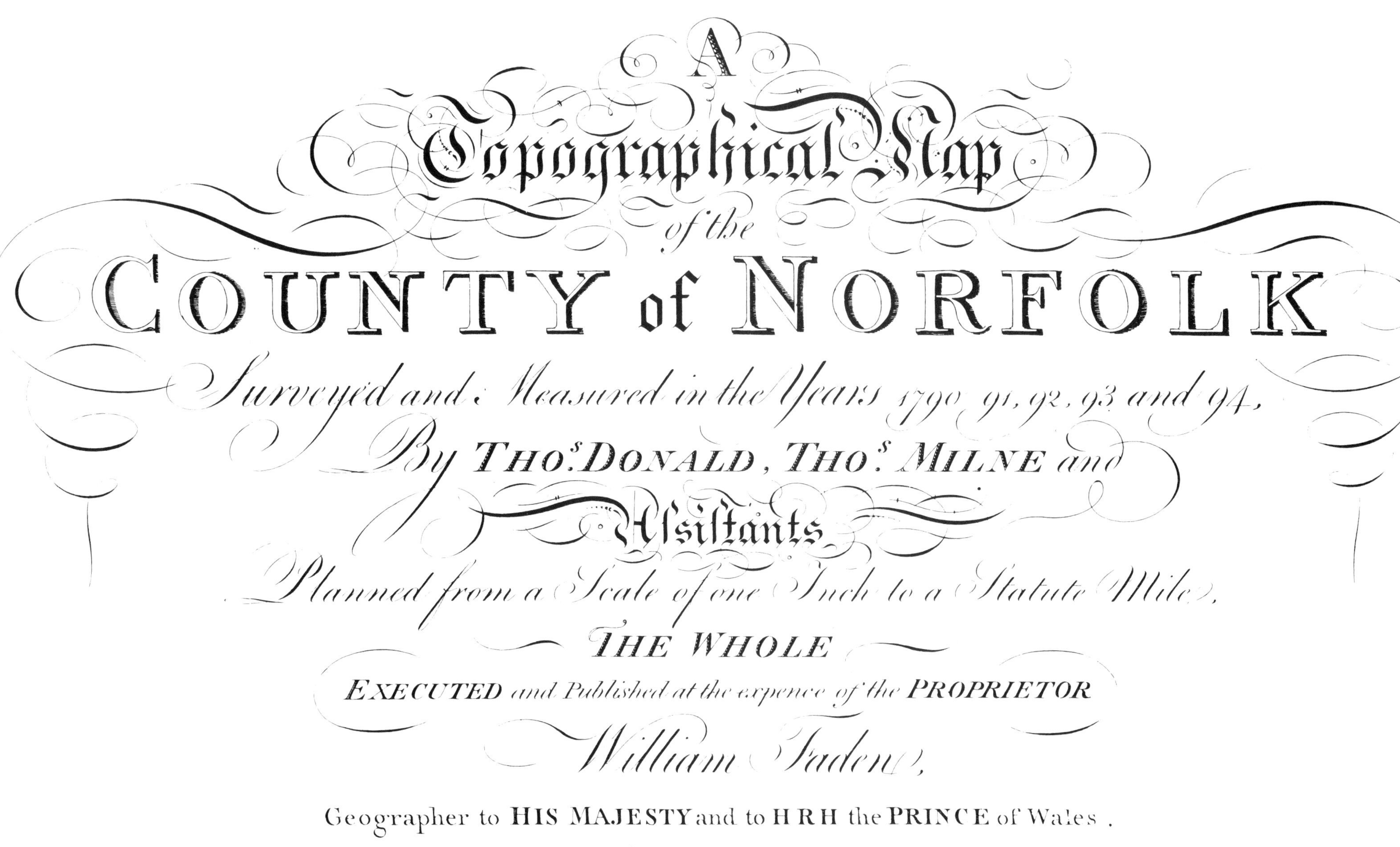

London August 12th 1797

Key

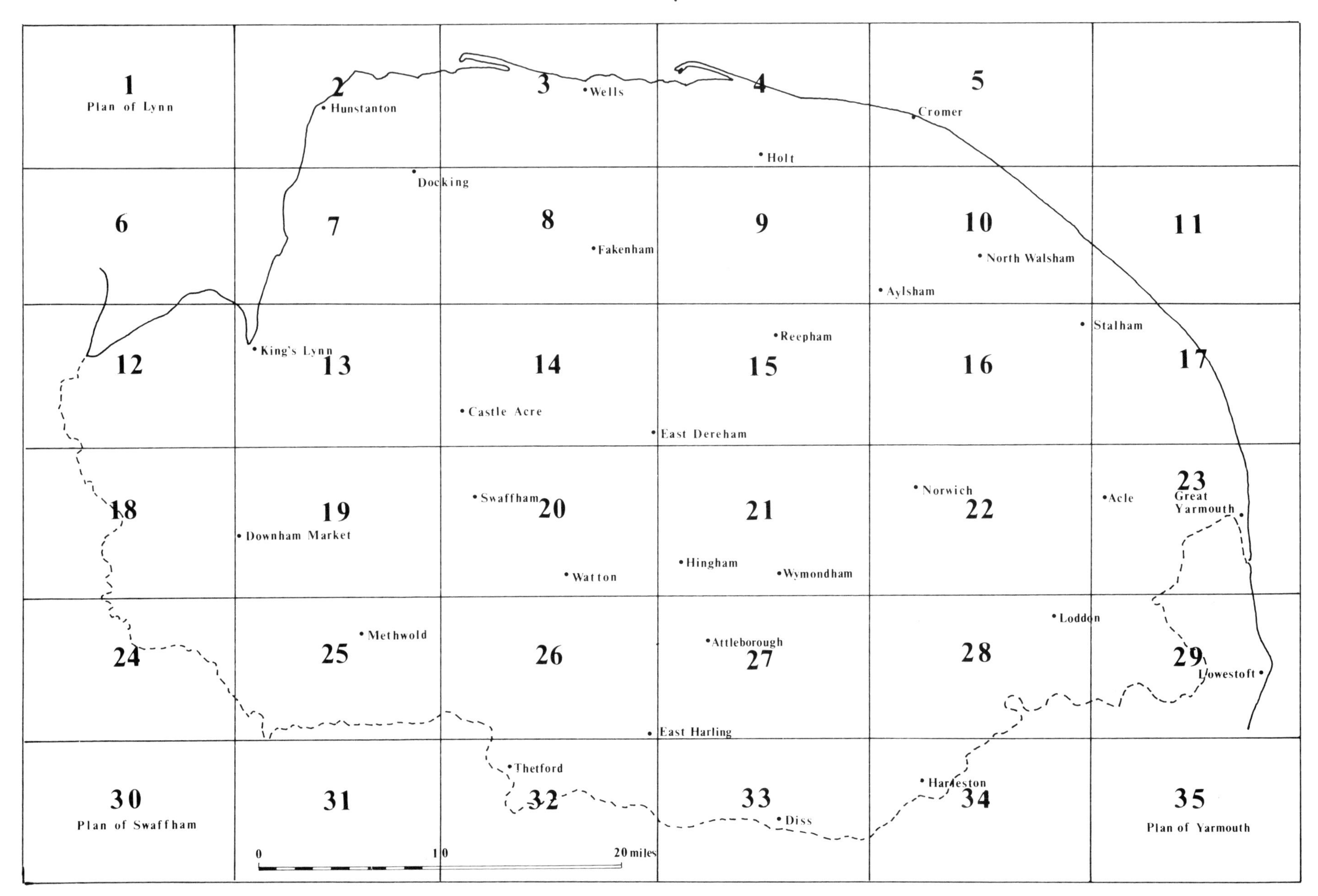

The town plans of Lynn and Great Yarmouth have been slightly reduced.

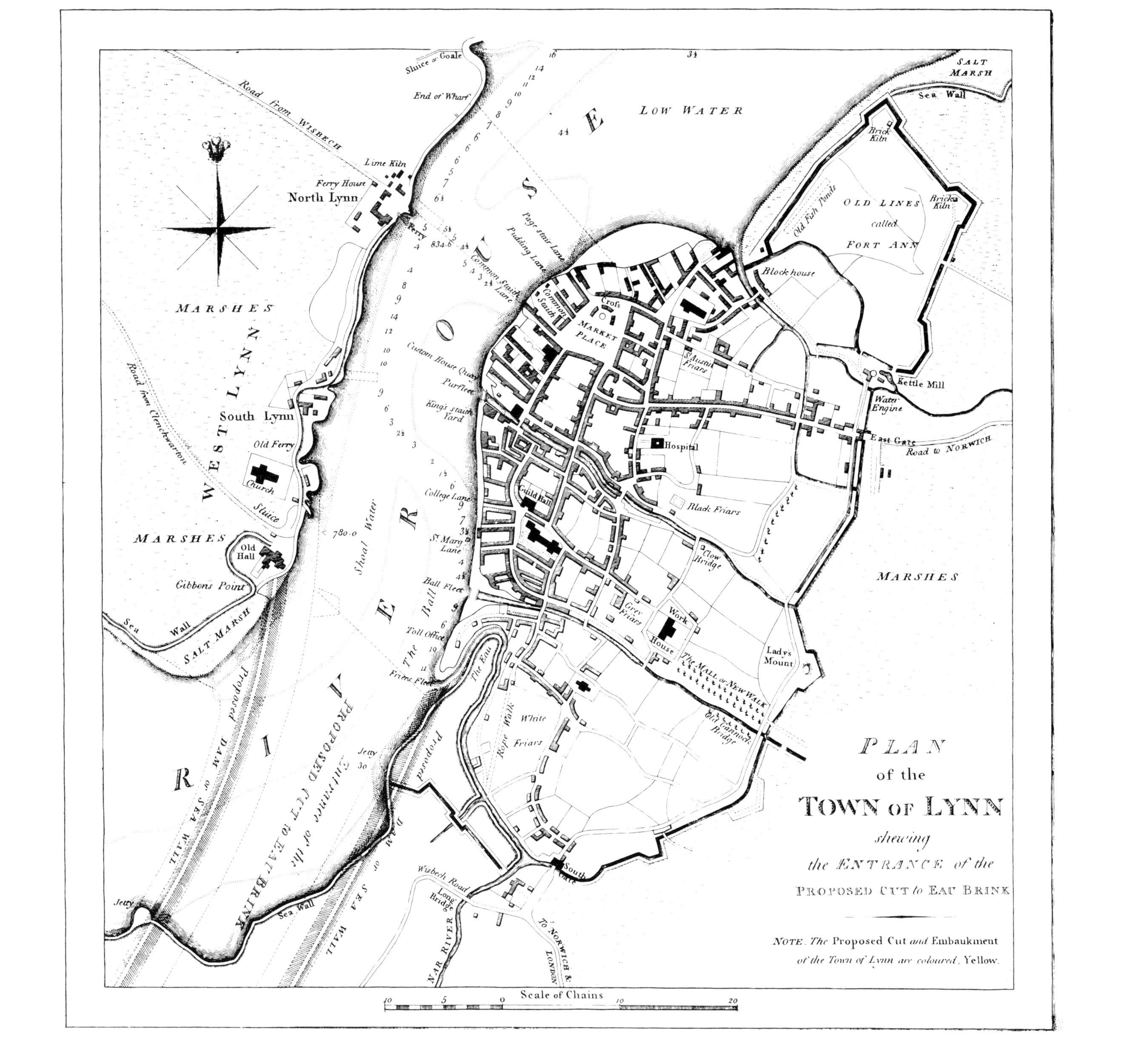
PLAN
of the
TOWN OF LYNN
shewing
the ENTRANCE of the
PROPOSED CUT to EAU BRINK
NOTE: The Proposed Cut and Embankment
of the Town of Lynn are coloured, Yellow.
Scale of Chains
RIVER OUSE
LOW WATER
SALT MARSH
Sea Wall
Brick Kiln
OLD LINES called FORT ANN
Old Fish Ponds
Block house
Kettle Mill
Water Engine
East Gate
Road to NORWICH
MARSHES
Hospital
Black Friars
Clow Bridge
Work House
Grey Friars
Ladys Mount
The MALL or NEW WALK
Old Cannock Bridge
White Friars
Rope Walk
The Eau
South Gate
Wisbech Road
Long Bridge
NAR RIVER
To NORWICH & LONDON
Sea Wall
DAM or SEA WALL
PROPOSED CUT to EAU BRINK
Entrance of the
Proposed
Jetty
Road from WISBECH
Sluice or Goale
End of Wharf
Lime Kiln
Ferry House
North Lynn
Ferry
MARSHES
WEST LYNN
Road from Clenchwarton
South Lynn
Old Ferry
Church
Sluice
Old Hall
Gibbons Point
SALT MARSH
Shoal Water
The Ball
Page stair Lane
Pudding Lane
Common Staith Lane
Common Staith
Cross
MARKET PLACE
St. Austin Friars
Custom House Quay
Purfleet
King's staith Yard
College Lane
Guild Hall
St. Marg. Lane
Ball Fleet
Toll Office
Friers Fleet

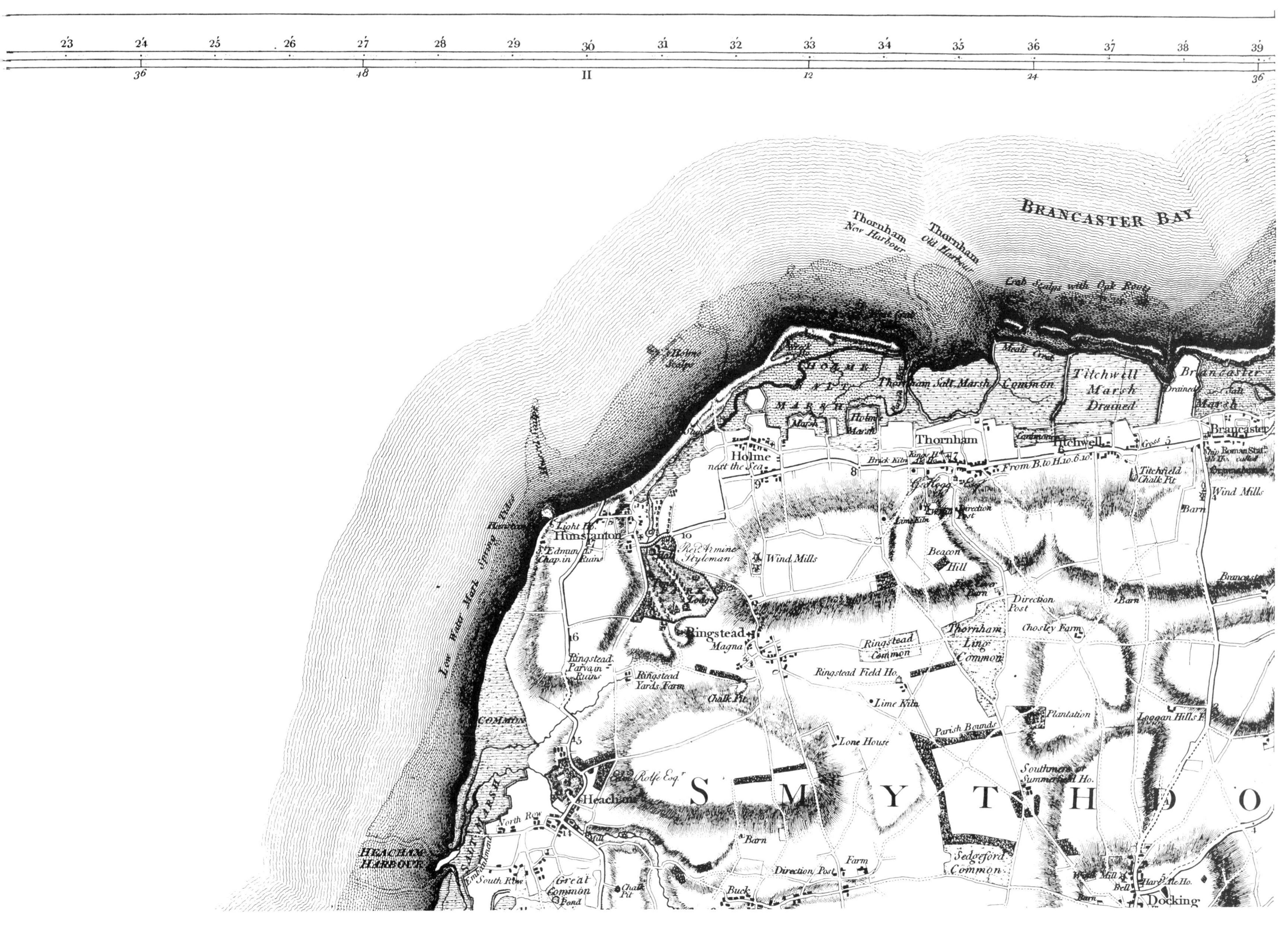

23
24
25
26
27
28
29
30
31
32
33
34
35
36
37
38
39
36
48
II
12
24
36
Brancaster Bay
Thornham
Thornham New Harbour
Thornham Old Harbour
Holme Scalps
Holme Salt Marsh
Marsh
Holme Marsh
Thornham Salt Marsh
Common
Meals Creek
Titchwell Marsh Drained
Brancaster Salt Marsh
Drained
Brancaster
Common
Titchwell
Gross 5
Thornham
Holme next the Sea
Brick Kiln
From B. to H. 10. 6. 10.
Titchfield Chalk Pit
Wind Mills
Barn
Direction Post
Lime Kiln
Light Ho.
Hunstanton
10
Rev. Armine Styleman
Wind Mills
Beacon Hill
St. Edmunds Chap. in Ruins
Lodge
Direction Post
Barn
Low Water Mark Spring Tides
Ringstead Magna
Ringstead Common
Thornham Ling Common
Chosley Farm
16
Ringstead Parva in Ruins
Ringstead Yards Farm
Chalk Pit
Ringstead Field Ho.
Lime Kiln
Plantation
Loggan Hills F.
Common
Parish Bounds
Lone House
15
Southmere or Summerfield Ho.
Rolfe Esq.
S M Y T H D O
Heacham
North Row
Barn
Heacham Harbour
Salt Marsh
Embankment
South Row
Great Common
Pond
Chalk Pit
Direction Post
Farm
Buck
Sedgeford Common
Wind Mill
Bell
Hare Ale Ho.
Barn
Docking

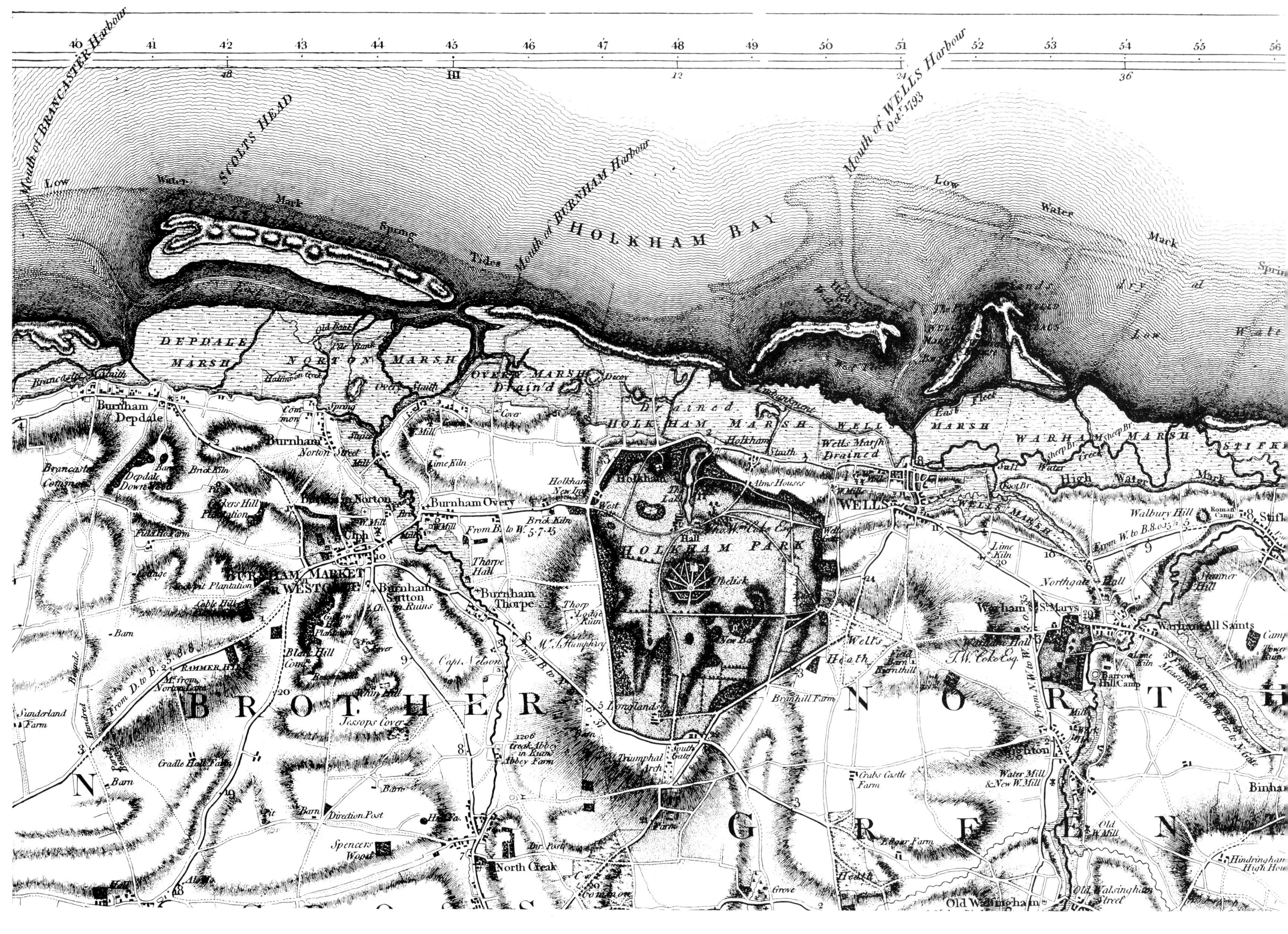

Mouth of BRANCASTER Harbour
SCOLTS HEAD
Mouth of BURNHAM Harbour
HOLKHAM BAY
Mouth of WELLS Harbour Octr. 1793
Low Water Mark
Spring Tides
DEPDALE MARSH
NORTON MARSH
OVERY MARSH Drain'd
HOLKHAM MARSH
WELL MARSH
WARHAM MARSH
High Water Mark
Burnham Depdale
Burnham Norton
Burnham Overy
BURNHAM MARKET
Burnham Sutton
Burnham Thorpe
Holkham
HOLKHAM PARK
Obelisk
WELLS
Wells Heath
Warham St. Marys
Warham All Saints
Northgate Hall
Walbury Hill
Brancaster Common
Lime Kiln
Thorpe Hall
Capt. Nelson
Longlands
Triumphal Arch
Creak Abbey in Ruins
North Creak
Spencers Wood
Direction Post
Jessops Cover
Sunderland Farm
Gradle Hall Farm
Branthill Farm
Grabs Castle Farm
Egmere Farm
Barrow Hill Camp
Old Walsingham
BROTHER
NORTH
GREEN

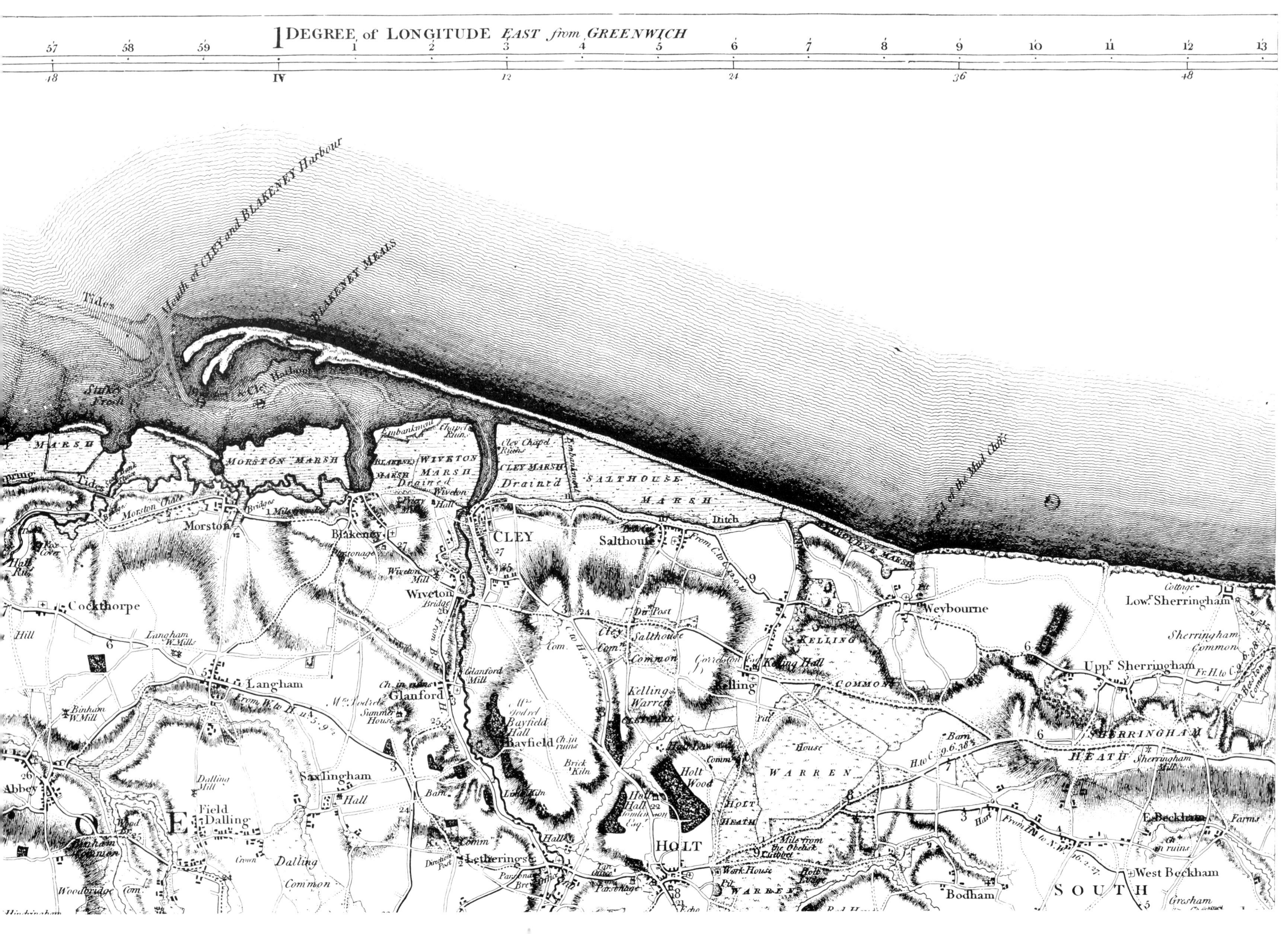

DEGREE of LONGITUDE EAST from GREENWICH
Mouth of CLEY and BLAKENEY Harbour
BLAKENEY MEALS
Tides
MARSH
MORSTON MARSH
WIVETON MARSH
Drained
CLEY MARSH
SALTHOUSE MARSH
Cley Chapel Ruins
Embankment
Morston
Blakeney
Parsonage
Wiveton
Wiveton Mill
Wiveton Bridge
CLEY
Salthouse
Ditch
Weybourne
Low.r Sherringham
Upp.r Sherringham
Sherringham Common
SHERRINGHAM
HEATH
Cockthorpe
Langham
Langham W.Mills
Binham W.Mill
Glanford
Glanford Mill
Bayfield Hall
Bayfield
Brick Kiln
Kelling
Kelling Hall
KELLING
COMMON
Kelling Warren
Salthouse Common
Holt Wood
Holt Hall
HOLT HEATH
WARREN
HOLT
Saxlingham
Hall
Field Dalling
Dalling Common
Letheringsett
Work House
Bodham
E.Beckham
West Beckham
SOUTH
Farms
Abbey
Hill

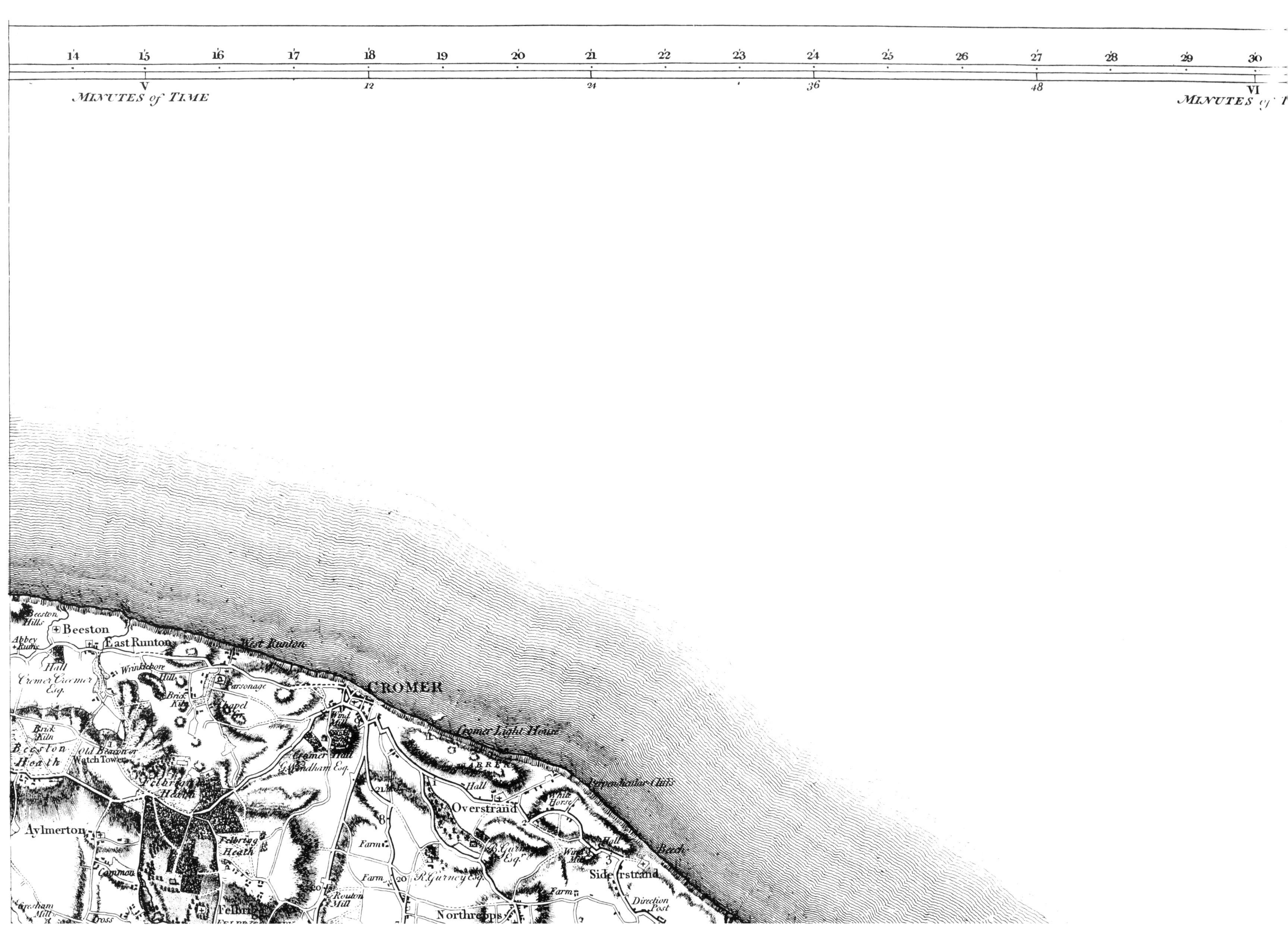
14
15
16
17
18
19
20
21
22
23
24
25
26
27
28
29
30
V
12
24
36
48
VI
MINUTES of TIME
Beeston Hills
Beeston
Abbey Ruins
East Runton
West Runton
Hall
Cromer Cromer Esq.
Wrinklebore Hill
Brick Kiln
Parsonage
CROMER
Chapel
Brick Kiln
Beeston Heath
Old Beacon or Watch Tower
Cromer Hall
G. Wyndham Esq.
Cromer Light House
Felbrigg Heath
Hall
Overstrand
Perpendicular Cliffs
White Horse
Aylmerton
Farm
Felbrigg Heath
Hall
Beach
Common
Farm
R. Gurney Esq.
Sidestrand
Routon Mill
Farm
Direction Post
Gresham Mill
Cross
Felbrigg
Northrepps

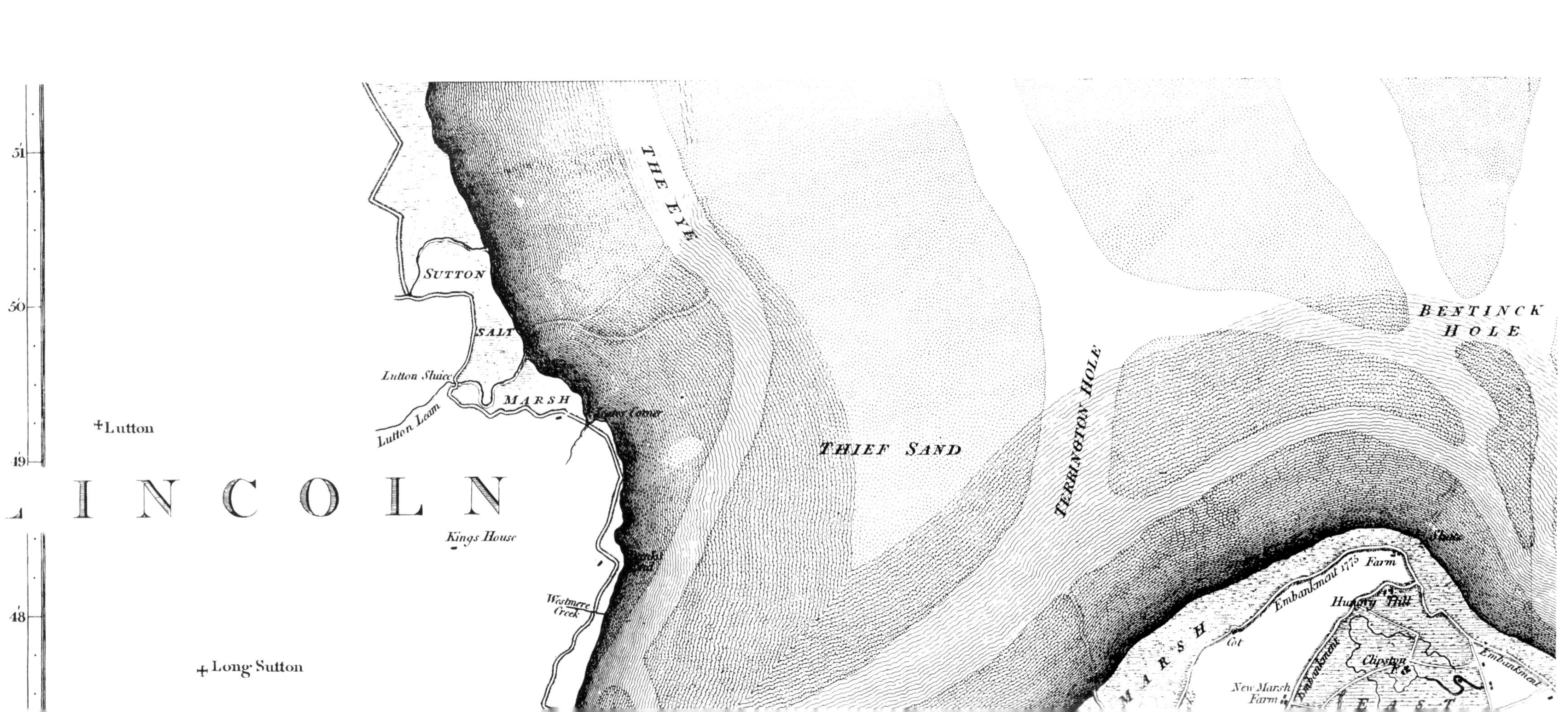
51
50
49
48
THE EYE
SUTTON
SALT
MARSH
Lutton Sluice
Lutton Leam
Lutton
LINCOLN
Kings House
Long Sutton
Westmere Creek
THIEF SAND
TERRINGTON HOLE
BENTINCK HOLE
Embankment 1775
Farm
Hungry Hill
Cot
MARSH
Clipston
Embankment
New Marsh Farm

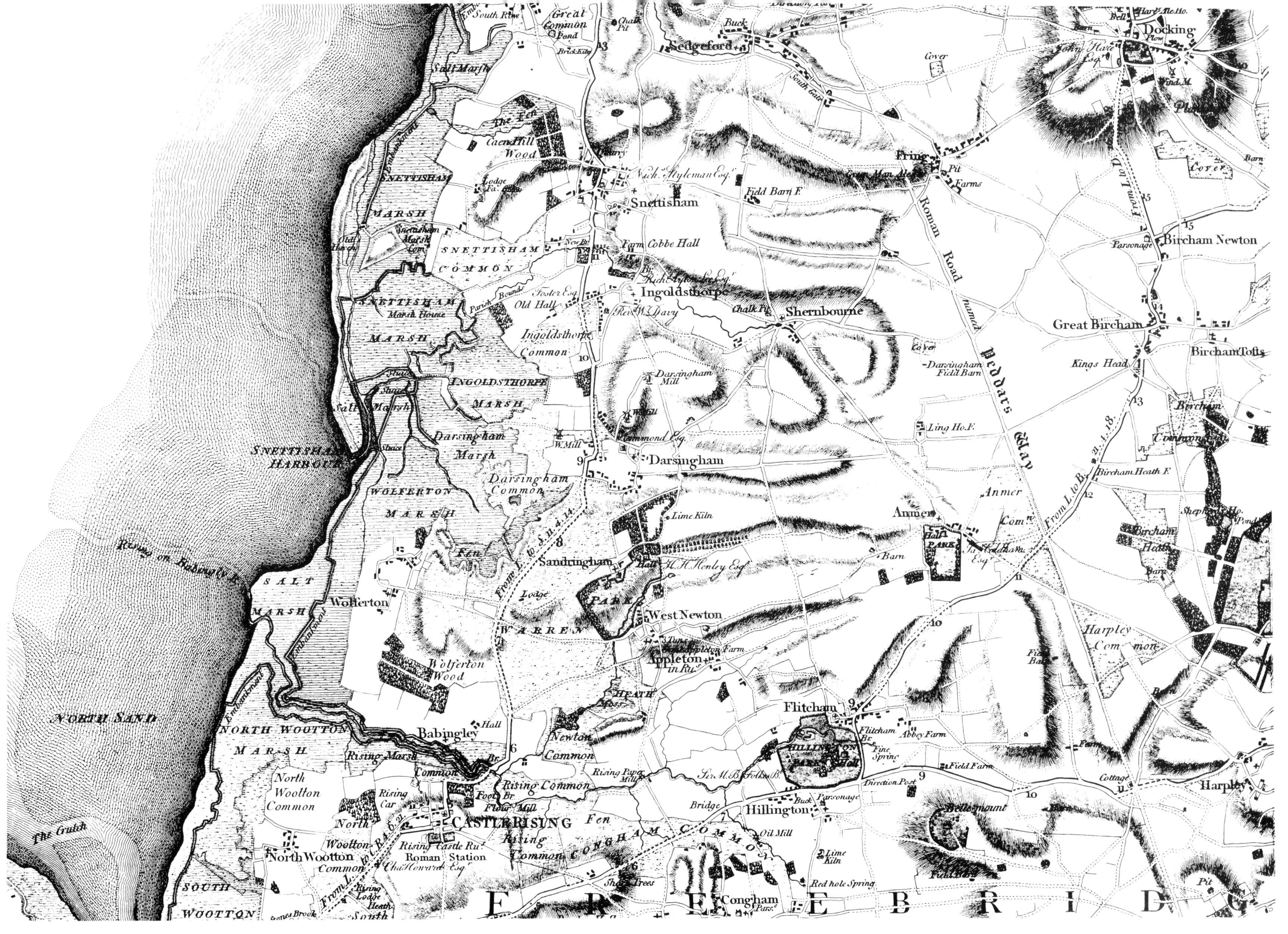

Sedgeford
Docking
Snettisham
SNETTISHAM
MARSH
SNETTISHAM
COMMON
Cobbe Hall
Ingoldsthorpe
Old Hall
Ingoldsthorpe
Common
Shernbourne
Chalk Pit
Fring
Pit
Farms
Fild Barn F.
Roman Road
named
Peddars Way
Bircham Newton
Parsonage
Great Bircham
Bircham Tofts
Kings Head
INGOLDSTHORPE
MARSH
Salt Marsh
SNETTISHAM
HARBOUR
Darsingham
Marsh
Darsingham
Darsingham
Common
Darsingham
Mill
W.Mill
Ling Ho.F.
WOLFERTON
MARSH
Fen
Lime Kiln
Anmer
Bircham Heath F.
Sandringham
Hall
H.H.Henley Esq.
PARK
Lodge
West Newton
WARREN
Wolferton
SALT
MARSH
Wolferton
Wood
Appleton
Harpley
Common
NORTH SAND
NORTH WOOTTON
MARSH
Babingley
Hall
Flitcham
Flitcham
Abbey Farm
Fine
Spring
Field Farm
Direction Post
Newton
Common
Rising Common
Rising Marsh
Common
North
Wootton
Common
CASTLERISING
Hillington
Parsonage
Bridge
Oil Mill
Lime
Kiln
Red hole Spring
Cottage
Harpley
The Gutch
North Wootton
Common
Rising Castle Ru.
Roman Station
Congham
SOUTH
WOOTTON
F R E E B R I D G

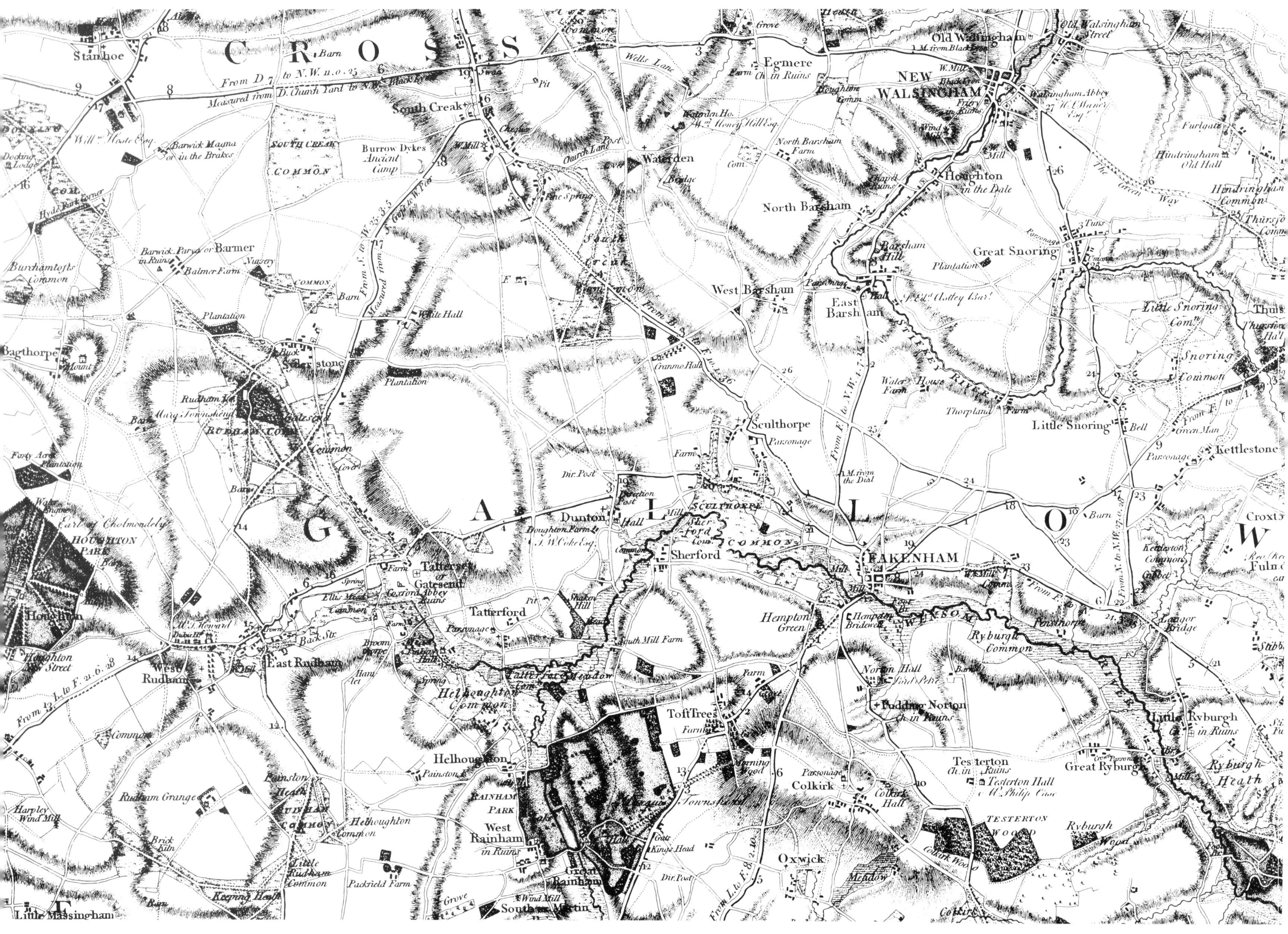
CROSS
GALLOW
Stanhoe
South Creak
Waterden
Egmere
NEW WALSINGHAM
Old Walsingham
Houghton in the Dale
North Barsham
West Barsham
East Barsham
Great Snoring
Little Snoring
Kettlestone
Sculthorpe
Dunton
Sherford
FAKENHAM
Tattersett or Gatesend
Tatterford
East Rudham
West Rudham
Houghton
Hempton Green
Toft Trees
Pudding Norton
Helhoughton
West Rainham in Ruins
Colkirk
Oxwick
Testerton
Great Ryburgh
Little Ryburgh in Ruins
Bagthorpe
Barwick Magna
Barmer
Burrow Dykes Ancient Camp
Thorpland
Rudham Grange
Harpley Wind Mill
Little Massingham
Packfield Farm
Testerton Wood
Ryburgh Wood
Ryburgh Common
Ryburgh Heath
Hindringham Old Hall
Hindringham Common
Little Snoring Com.
Snoring Common
Kettlestone Common
Pensthorpe
Langer Bridge
Sculthorpe Common
South Mill Farm
Norton Hall
Colkirk Hall
Townshend
Morning Wood
Painston
Rainham Park
Helhoughton Common
Little Rudham Common
Rudham Common
Houghton Park
Earl of Cholmondeley
Forty Acre Plantation
Burchamtofts Common
Docking Lodge
Hyde Park Corner
Plantation
White Hall
Waterden Ho.
North Barsham Farm
Barsham Hill
Great Rainham
South Martin
Kings Head
Hempton Bridewell
Stiffkey River
Wenson River
Egmere Ch. in Ruins
Walsingham Abbey
Furlgate
The Green Way

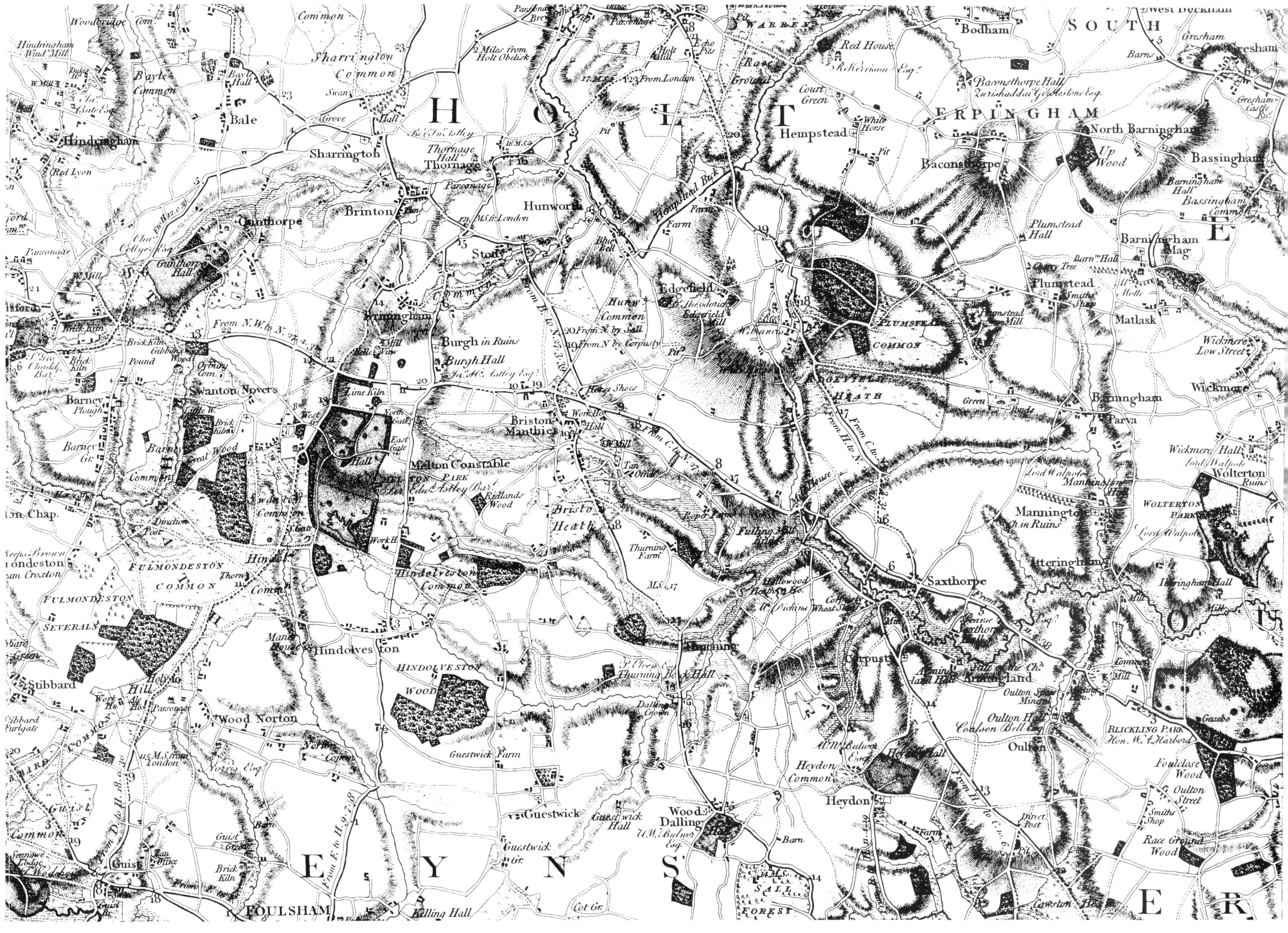

HOLT
ERPINGHAM
SOUTH
EYNSFORD
Sharrington Common
Sharrington
Bayle Common
Bayle Hall
Bale
Hindringham
Hindringham Wind Mill
Woodbridge Com.
Red Lyon
Gunthorpe
Gunthorpe Hall
Brinton
Thornage Hall
Thornage
Parsonage
Hunworth
Stody
Briningham
Belle View
Burgh in Ruins
Burgh Hall
Swanton Novers
Lime Kiln
Melton Constable
Briston
Mauthies
Work Ho. Hall
Edgefield
Edgefield Mill
Hempstead
Court Green
Red House
Bodham
Baconsthorpe Hall
Baconsthorpe
North Barningham
Up Wood
Bassingham
Barningham Hall
Plumstead Hall
Barningham Mag
Plumstead
Plumstead Mill
Plumstead Common
Matlask
Wickmere Low Street
Wickmere
Barningham Parva
Wickmere Hall
Wolterton
Wolterton Ruins
Wolterton Park
Lord Walpole
Mannington
Mannington Hall
Saxthorpe
Itteringham
Itteringham Hall
Corpusty
Aldborough
Oulton Hall
Oulton
Blickling Park
Hon. W. A. Harbord
Foulclose Wood
Oulton Street
Smiths Shop
Race Ground Wood
Heydon Hall
Heydon Common
Heydon
Wood Dalling
Thurning
Thurning Hall
Thurning Farm
Briston Heath
Hindolveston Common
Hindolveston
Hindolveston Wood
Guestwick Farm
Guestwick
Guestwick Hall
Wood Norton
Fulmondeston Common
Fulmondeston Severals
Stibbard
Stibbard Furlgate
Holy Ho. Hill
Guist
Guist Common
Brick Kiln
Foulsham
Kelling Hall
Sall Forest
Cawston
Barney
Barney Plough
Barney Gr.
Great Wood
Swanton Common
Ridlands Wood
Hempstead Beck
From London
Race Ground
Gresham
Gresham Castle Ruins
Barns
West Beckham
Blue Bell
Hunw. Common
Fulling Mill Bridge
Cot Gr.
Direction Post

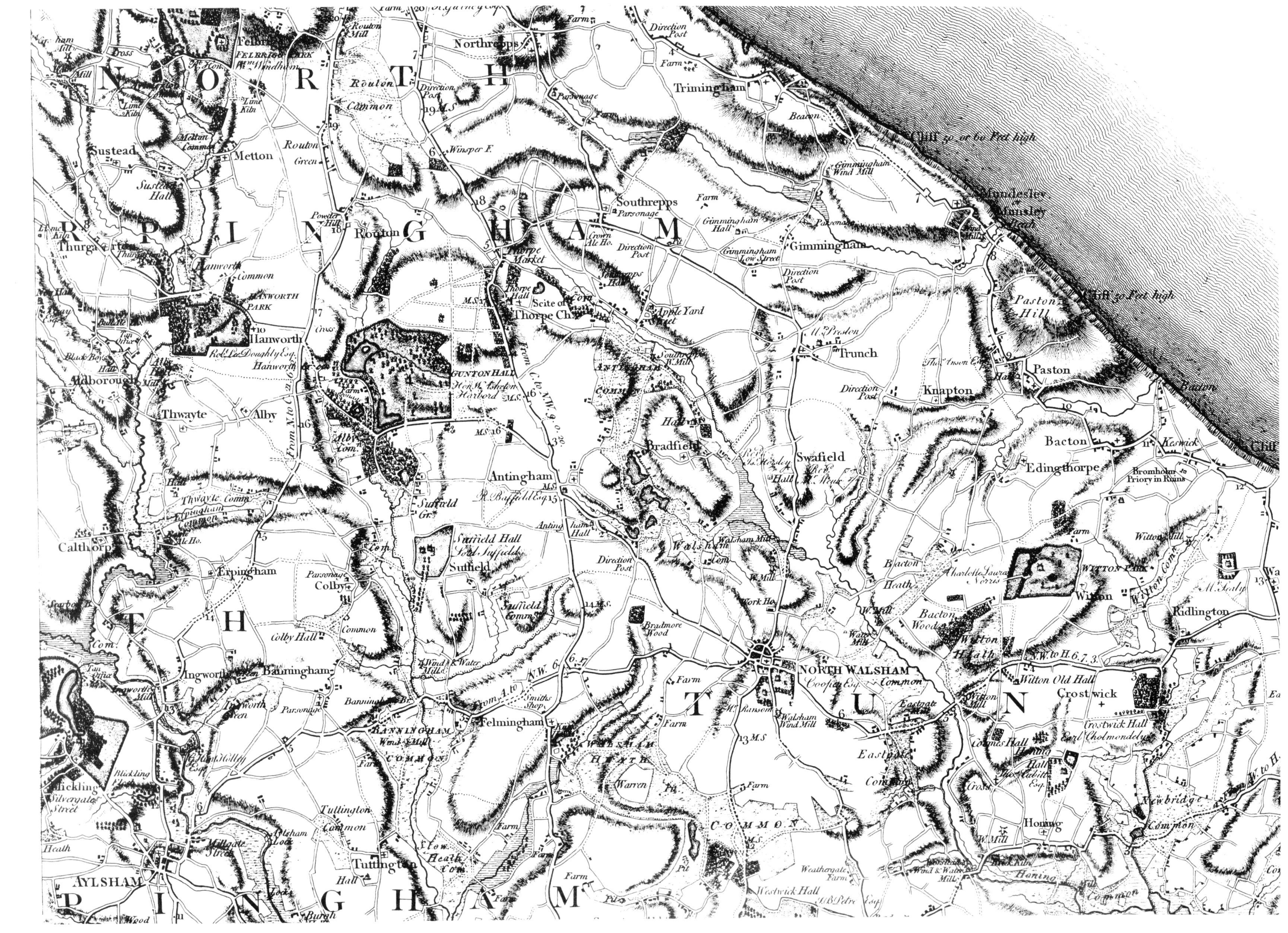

NORTH
REPPINGHAM
TUN
ERPINGHAM
Northrepps
Trimingham
Felbrigg
Sustead
Metton
Routon
Southrepps
Gimmingham
Mundesley
Thurgarton
Hanworth
Thorpe Market
Trunch
Paston
Knapton
Aldborough
Thwayte
Alby
Gunton Hall
Bradfield
Swafield
Bacton
Edingthorpe
Antingham
Calthorp
Erpingham
Colby
Suffield
Witton
Ridlington
Ingworth
Bannigham
Felmingham
North Walsham
Crostwick
Blickling
Aylsham
Tuttington
Honing
Newbridge
Cliff 50 or 60 Feet high
Cliff 50 Feet high
Bromholm Priory in Ruins
Witton Park
Bacton Wood
Bradmore Wood
Westwick Hall

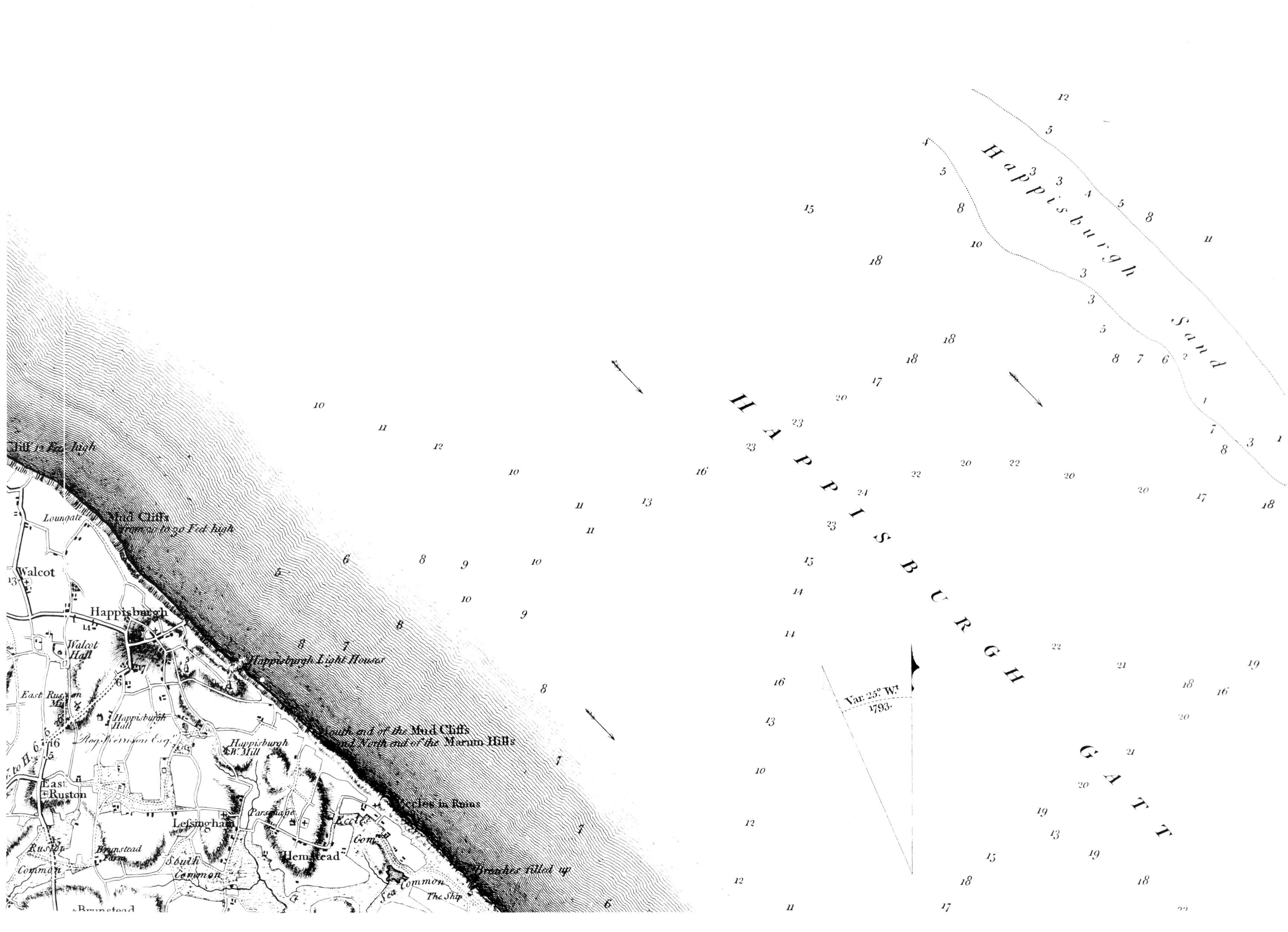

Happisburgh Sand
HAPPISBURGH
HAPPISBURGH GATT
Var. 25° Wt 1793.
Cliff 12 Feet high
Mud Cliffs
from 20 to 30 Feet high
Loungate
Walcot
Happisburgh
Walcot Hall
Happisburgh Light Houses
East Ruston Mill
Happisburgh Hall
South end of the Mud Cliffs
and North end of the Marum Hills
Happisburgh W. Mill
East Ruston
Lessingham
Parsonage
Eccles in Ruins
Ruston Common
Brunstead Farm
South Common
Hemstead
Breaches filled up
Sea Common
The Ship
Brunstead

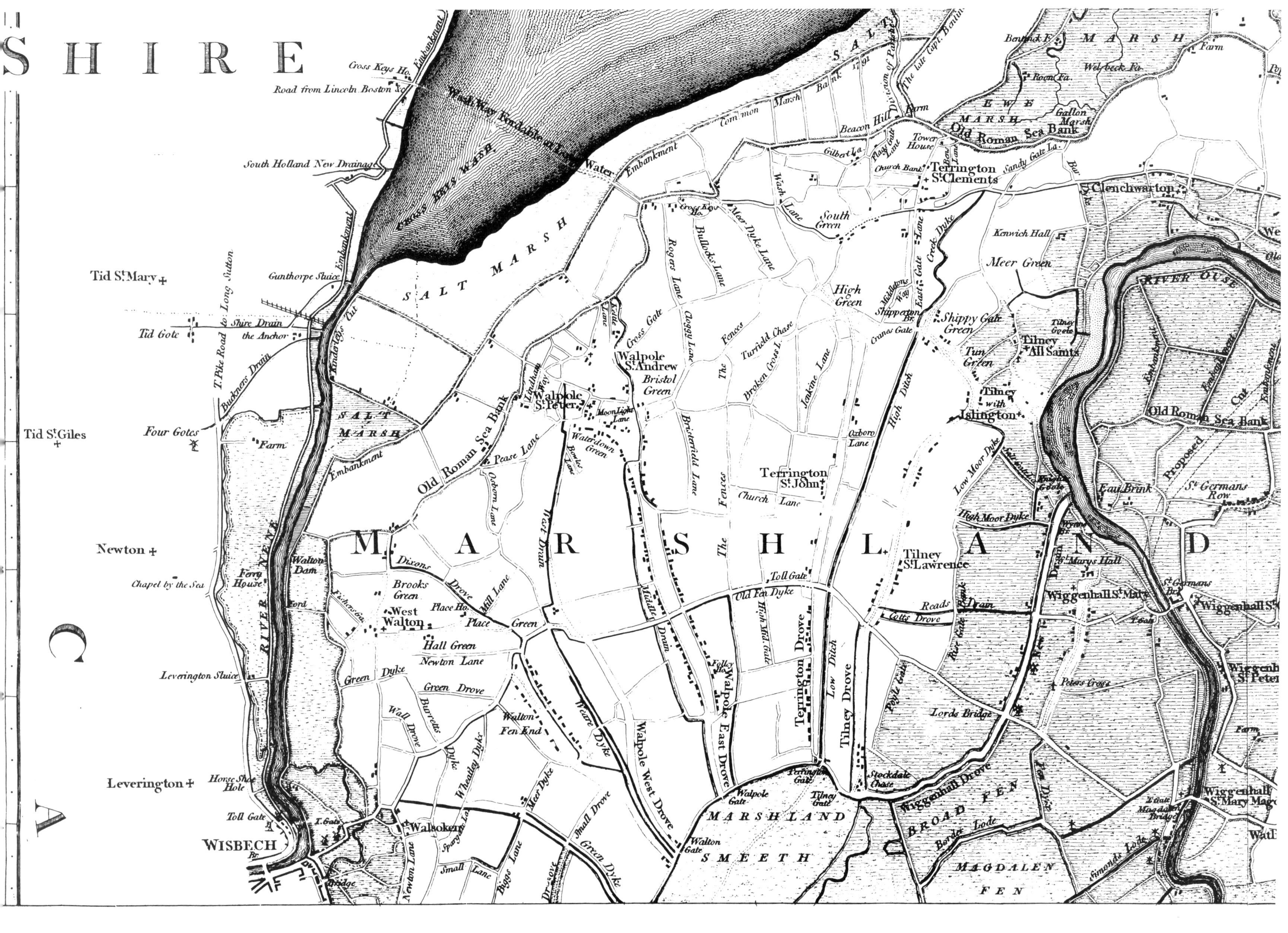

SHIRE
MARSHLAND
SALT MARSH
Gross Keys Ho.
Embankment
Road from Lincoln Boston &c.
South Holland New Drainage
Wash Way Fordable at Low Water
Tid St. Mary
Gunthorpe Sluice
Tid Gote
Shire Drain
the Anchor
T. Pike Road to Long Sutton
Buckners Drain
Four Gotes
Farm
Tid St. Giles
Newton
Chapel by the Sea
Ferry House
Walton Dam
RIVER NENE
Leverington Sluice
Leverington
Horse Shoe Hole
Toll Gate
WISBECH
Br.
Walsoken
West Walton
Brooks Green
Dixons Drove
Mill Lane
Place Ho.
Place Green
Hall Green
Newton Lane
Green Dyke
Green Drove
Wall Drove
Burretts Dyke
Wheatley Dyke
Walton Fen End
Meer Dyke
Small Drove
Green Dyke
Small Lane
Biggs Lane
Newton Lane
Old Roman Sea Bank
Pease Lane
Osborn Lane
West Drain
Weare Dyke
Walpole West Drove
Walpole St. Peter
Walpole St. Andrew
Bristol Green
Moon Light Lane
Waterdown Green
Gross Gate
Rogers Lane
Bullocks Lane
Meer Dyke Lane
Cloggy Lane
Briarfield Lane
Middle Drain
Walpole East Drove
Folley Ho.
The Fences
Turfield Chase
Broken Cross L.
Jenkins Lane
Terrington St. John
Church Lane
Old Fen Dyke
Toll Gate
High Mill Gate
Terrington Drove
Low Ditch
Tilney Drove
Terrington Gate
Walpole Gate
Tilney Gate
Walton Gate
MARSHLAND SMEETH
Stockdale Chase
High Green
High Ditch
Oxboro Lane
Cranes Gate
Shipperton Br.
East Gate Lane
Creek Dyke
Wash Lane
South Green
Church Bank
Gilbert La.
Terrington St. Clements
Beacon Hill Farm
Tower House
Common Marsh Bank 1791
Sandy Gate La.
Clenchwarton
Kenwich Hall
Meer Green
Shippy Gate Green
Tun Green
Tilney All Saints
Tilney Gote
Tilney with Islington
Low Moor Dyke
High Moor Dyke
Tilney St. Lawrence
Reads Drain
Cotts Drove
Pople Gate
Lords Bridge
Wiggenhall Drove
BROAD FEN
Border Lode
MAGDALEN FEN
Simonds Lode
Old Roman Sea Bank
EWE MARSH
Welbeck Fa.
Gallon Marsh
Farm
RIVER OUSE
Eau Brink
St. Germans Row
Proposed Cut
Embankment
St. Marys Hall
Wiggenhall St. Mary
St. Germans Br.
Wiggenhall St. Germans
Wiggenhall St. Peter
Peters Cross
Farm
Wiggenhall St. Mary Magdalen
Magdalen Bridge

Wootton Marsh
South Wootton
South Wootton Warren
Roydon Hall
Roydon
Roydon Row
Grimston Cross
Congham W. Mill
Congham Common
Popes Home
North Lynn
Gay Wood Common
Gaywood Common
Roydon Common
Grimston Warren
Grimston Common
Grimston
Pot Row
Bawsey in Ruins
Gaywood
Lynn Regis
West Lynn
Old Hall
Grimston Fen
Leziat Fen
Leziat in Ruins
Bawsey Common
Mintlyn Church in Ruins
Leziat Warren
Mintlyn Warren
Mintlyn
Brow of the Hill
Ash Wicken
Gayton
Gayton Common
Gaytonthorpe
Gaytonthorpe High Common
Great Massingham High Common
Great Massingham Com.
Gayton Common
Hardwick
Hardwick Green
Middleton Common
Middleton Tower in Ruins
Ferrets Hill Common
West Winch Common
West Winch
North Runcton
Middleton
East Winch
East Walton
West Bilney
E. Winch Heath
E. Winch Common
East Walton Common
Westacre
Westacre Hall
Westacre Chap. in Ruins
St. Germain
Setchy
Nar or Setchy River
Middleton Hithe
Bilney Heath
Pentney Heath
Bilney Lodge
Pentney
Pentney Common
Narford
Narford Hall
Wormegay Fen
Wormegay
Pentney Hall
Ruins of Pentney Abbey
Pentney Mill
Narborough
Narborough Hall
Roman Camp
Narborough Fen
Narr
Tottenhill
Tottenhill Heath
Marham Drain
Lynn

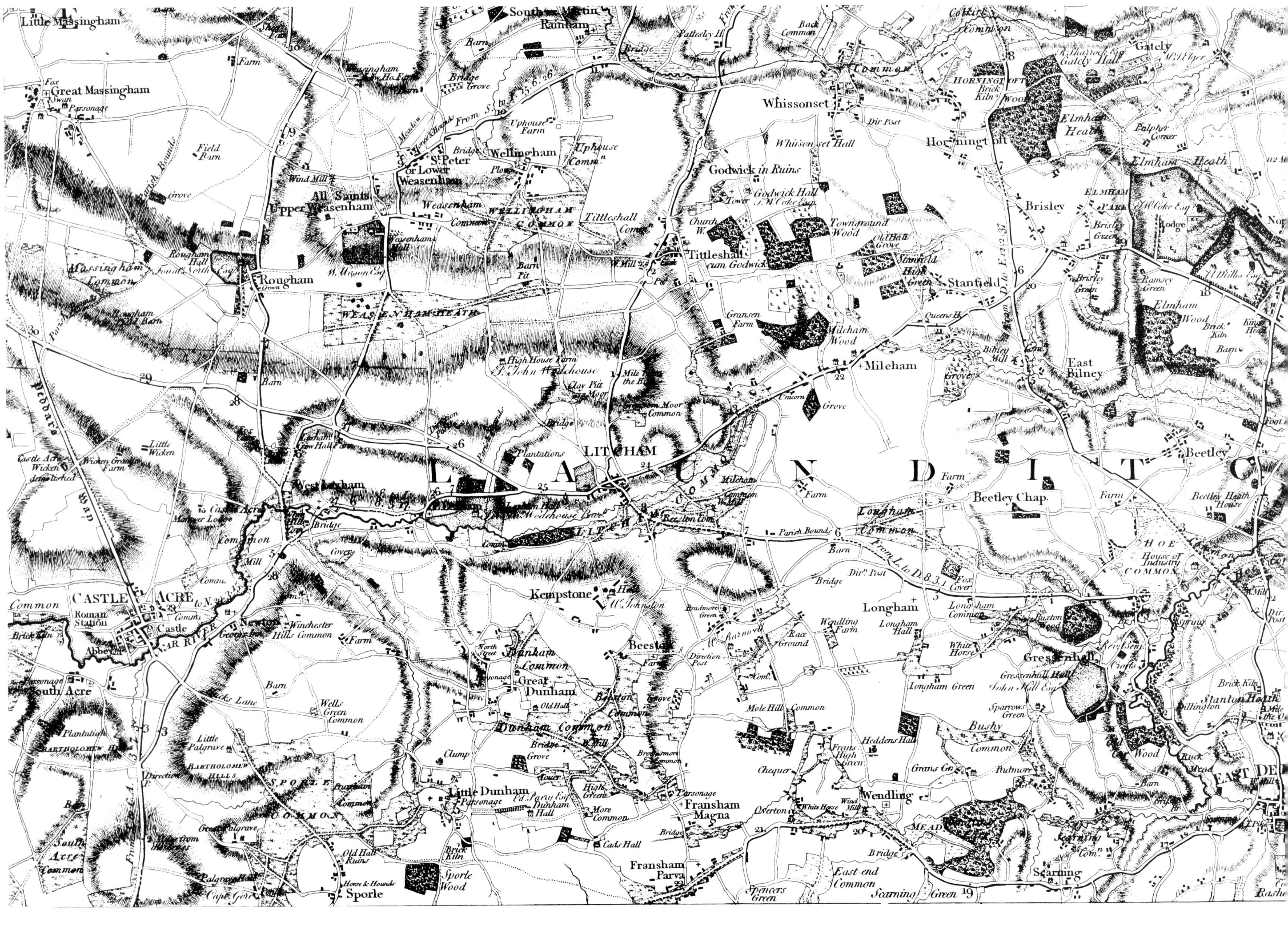

Little Massingham
Great Massingham
Parsonage
Farm
Field Barn
Grove
Wind Mill
All Saints
Upper Weasenham
St. Peter
or Lower
Weasenham
Wellingham
Uphouse Farm
Weasenham Common
WELLINGHAM COMMON
Tittleshall Comm.
Rougham Hall
Rougham
Massingham Common
WEASENHAM HEATH
Rainham
Bridge Grove
Bridge
Whissonset
Whisonset Hall
Godwick in Ruins
Godwick Hall
Tittleshall cum Godwick
Townground Wood
Gransen Farm
Milcham Wood
Mileham
Grove
Stanfield
Queens H.
Horningtoft
Gately
Gately Hall
Elmham Heath
Brisley
Brisley Green
ELMHAM PARK
Elmham Wood
Ramsey Green
East Bilney
Bilney Mill
High House Farm
Clay Pit Moor
Plantations
LITCHAM
Farm
Beetley Chap.
Beetley
Beetley Heath House
Longham Common
Parish Bounds
From L. to D. 8.3.1
West Lexham
Castle Acre Widen demolished
Little Wicken
Wicken Grange Farm
Bridge
Cover
Common
Mill
CASTLE ACRE
Roman Station
Castle
Abbey
NAR RIVER
Newton
Hills Common
Barn
Farm
Kempstone
Beeston
Beeston Common
Bradmore Green
Race Ground
Wendling Farm
Direction Post
Longham
Longham Hall
Longham Common
Longham Green
Buston Wood
White Horse
Gressenhall
Gressenhall Hall
John Hill Esq.
Stanton Heath
Bushy Common
Sparrows Green
Heddens Hall
Mole Hill Common
North Street
Dunham Common
Parsonage
Great Dunham
Old Hall
Wells Green Common
South Acre
Plantation
BARTHOLOMEW HILLS
Little Palgrave
SPORLE COMMON
Clump
Bridge Grove
Little Dunham
Parsonage
Dunham Hall
High Green
More Common
Cads Hall
Fransham Magna
Parsonage
Chequer
Overton
Wendling
Grans Gn.
Putmore
Great Palgrave
Old Hall Ruins
Brick Kiln
Sporle Wood
Sporle
Fransham Parva
Spencers Green
East end Common
Scarning Green
Scarning
Scarning Com.
EAST DE

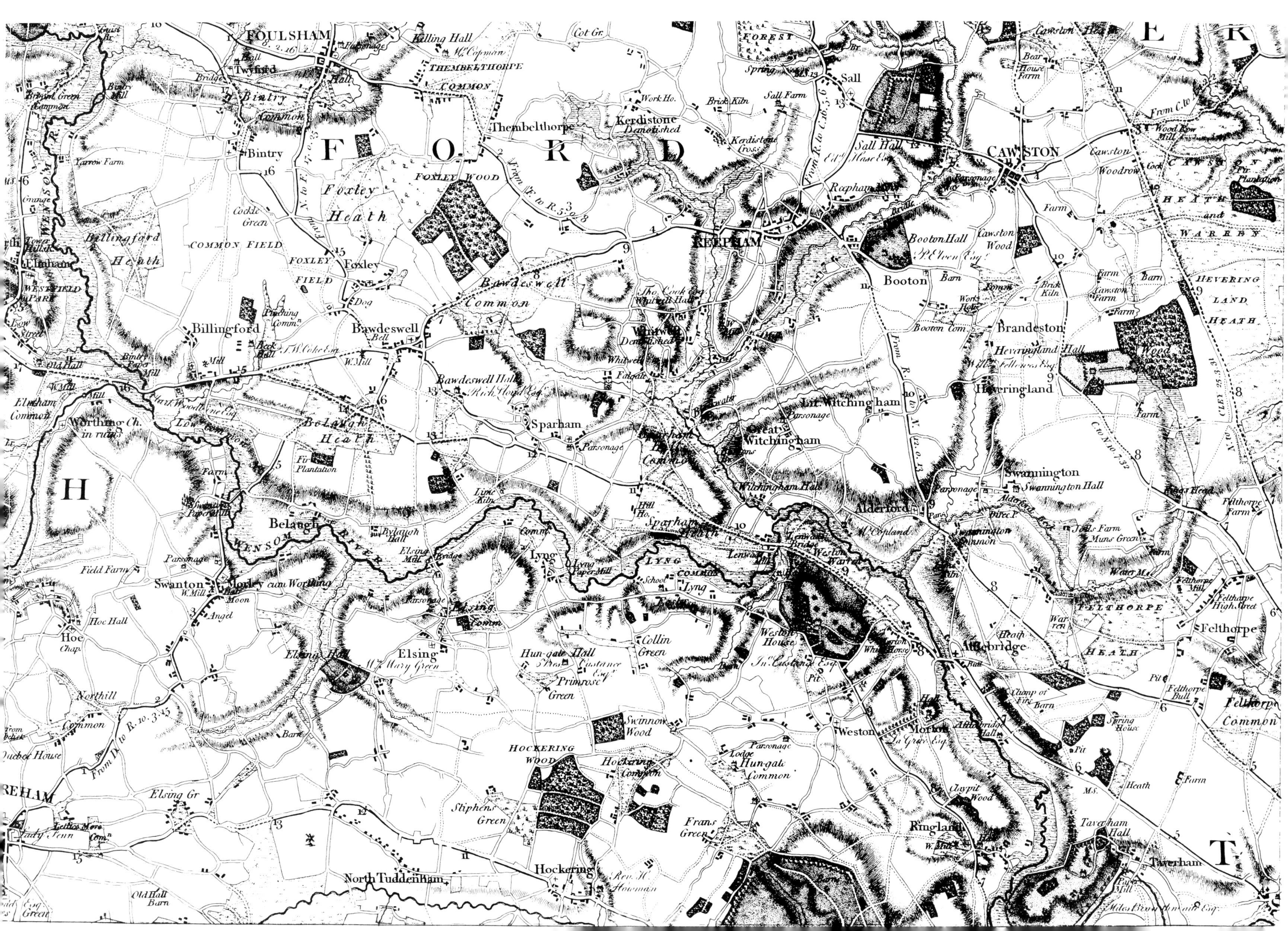

FOULSHAM
Killing Hall
THEMBELTHORPE
COMMON
Twyford
Bintry
Common
Thembelthorpe
Kerdistone
Demolished
Kerdistone Cross
Brick Kiln
Sall Farm
Sall
FOREST
Cawston Heath
Bear
House Farm
E
R
F
O
R
D
Bintry
Yarrow Farm
Foxley
Heath
FOXLEY WOOD
Sall Hall
CAWSTON
Cawston
Woodrow
Wood Row Mill
Fir Plantation
Reepham
Billingford
Heath
COMMON FIELD
FOXLEY
FIELD
Foxley
Bawdeswell
Common
REEPHAM
Booton Hall
Cawston Wood
HEATH
and
WARREN
Booton
HEVERINGLAND
HEATH
Whitwell Hall
Cawston Farm
Billingford
Bawdeswell
Whitwell
Demolished
Booton Com.
Brandeston
Heveringland Hall
Wood
Heveringland
Old Hall
Elmham Common
Worthing Ch.
in ruin
Low Com.
Belaugh
Heath
Bawdeswell Hall
Sparham
Parsonage
Lit. Witchingham
Great Witchingham
Swannington
Swannington Hall
H
Fir Plantation
Lime Kiln
Witchingham Hall
Alderford
Parsonage
Hill Ho.
Sparham Heath
Belaugh
WENSOM
RIVER
Bylaugh Hall
Lyng
Elsing Mill
Bridge
Lenwade Bridge
Weston Warren
Felthorpe Farm
Field Farm
Parsonage
Swanton
Morley cum Worthing
Lyng Paper Mill
LYNG
COMMON
School
Lyng
Felthorpe Mill
Felthorpe High Street
FELTHORPE
Hoe Hall
Hoe
Angel
Parsonage
Elsing
Comm.
Collin Green
Weston House
Attlebridge
Felthorpe
HEATH
Elsing Hall
Elsing
Hun-gate Hall
Primrose Green
Northill
Common
Barn
Swinnow Wood
Weston
Morton
Attlebridge Hall
Felthorpe Bull
Felthorpe Common
Quebec House
HOCKERING WOOD
Hockering Common
Hun-gate Common
Parsonage
Lodge
Claypit Wood
Heath
Farm
REHAM
Elsing Gr
Stiphens Green
Frans Green
Ringland
Taverham Hall
Taverham
T
North Tuddenham
Hockering
Old Hall Barn

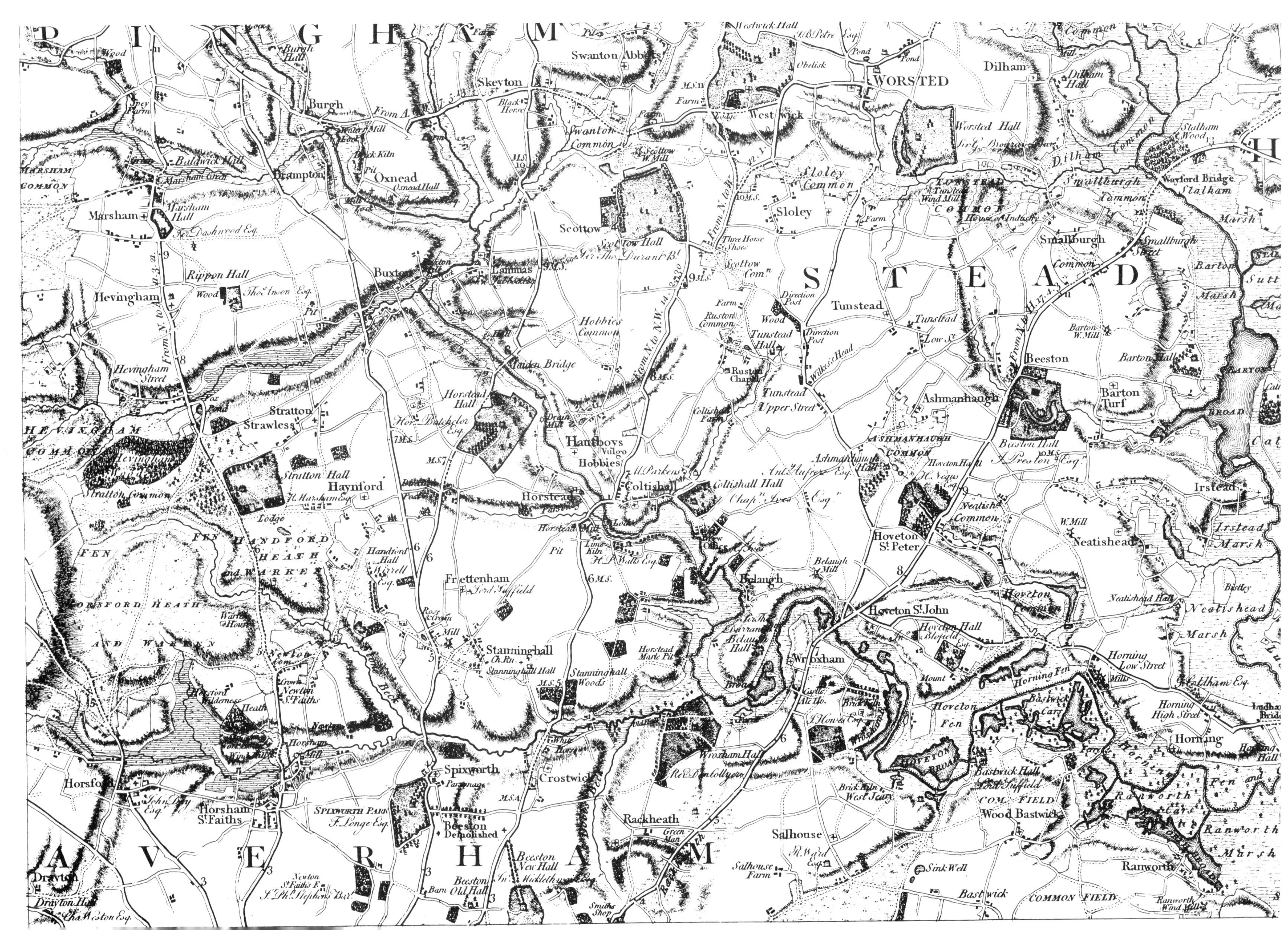

Swanton Abbots
Westwick Hall
Worsted
Dilham
Dilham Hall
Burgh Hall
Skeyton
Burgh
Westwick
Worsted Hall
Swanton Common
Oxnead
Oxnead Hall
Brampton
Baldwick Hall
Marsham Common
Marsham
Marsham Hall
Scottow
Scottow Hall
Sloley
Sloley Common
Tunstead Wind Mill
House of Industry
Smallburgh
Smallburgh Common
Wayford Bridge
Stalham
Stalham Common
Stalham Wood
Rippon Hall
Hevingham
Buxton
Lammas
Scottow Com.
Tunstead
Barton
Barton Marsh
Hobbies Common
Ruston Common
Tunstead Hall
Tunstead Low St.
Beeston
Barton W. Mill
Barton Hall
Hevingham Street
Maiden Bridge
Horstead Hall
Ruston Chapel
Tunstead Upper Street
Ashmanhaugh
Barton Turf
Hevingham Common
Stratton
Strawless
Hautboys
Hobbies
Ashmanhaugh Common
Beeston Hall
Stratton Hall
Haynford
Coltishall
Coltishall Hall
Irstead
Stratton Common
Horstead
Horstead Mill
Neatishead Common
Hoveton St. Peter
Neatishead
Irstead Marsh
Handford Heath and Warren
Handford Hall
Frettenham
Belaugh
Belaugh Mill
Neatishead Hall
Horsford Heath and Warren
Hoveton St. John
Hoveton Hall
Hoveton Common
Neatishead Marsh
Stanninghall
Stanninghall Hall
Horstead Marle Pit
Belaugh Hall
Wroxham
Horning Low Street
Horning Fen
Stanninghall Woods
Newton St. Faiths
Horsford Wilderness
Hoveton Fen
Bastwick Carr
Horning High Street
Horning
Horning Hall
Horsham Mill
Wroxham Hall
Hoveton Broad
Spixworth
Crostwick
Bastwick Hall
Horsford
Horsham St. Faiths
Spixworth Park
Rackheath
Com. Field
Wood Bastwick
Ranworth Carr
Ranworth Marsh
Beeston Demolished
Salhouse
Sink Well
Ranworth
Drayton
Drayton Hall
Beeston New Hall
Beeston Old Hall
Salhouse Farm
Bastwick
Common Field
Ranworth Wind Mill
Smiths Shop
Stanning Beck
Newton St. Faiths Bar

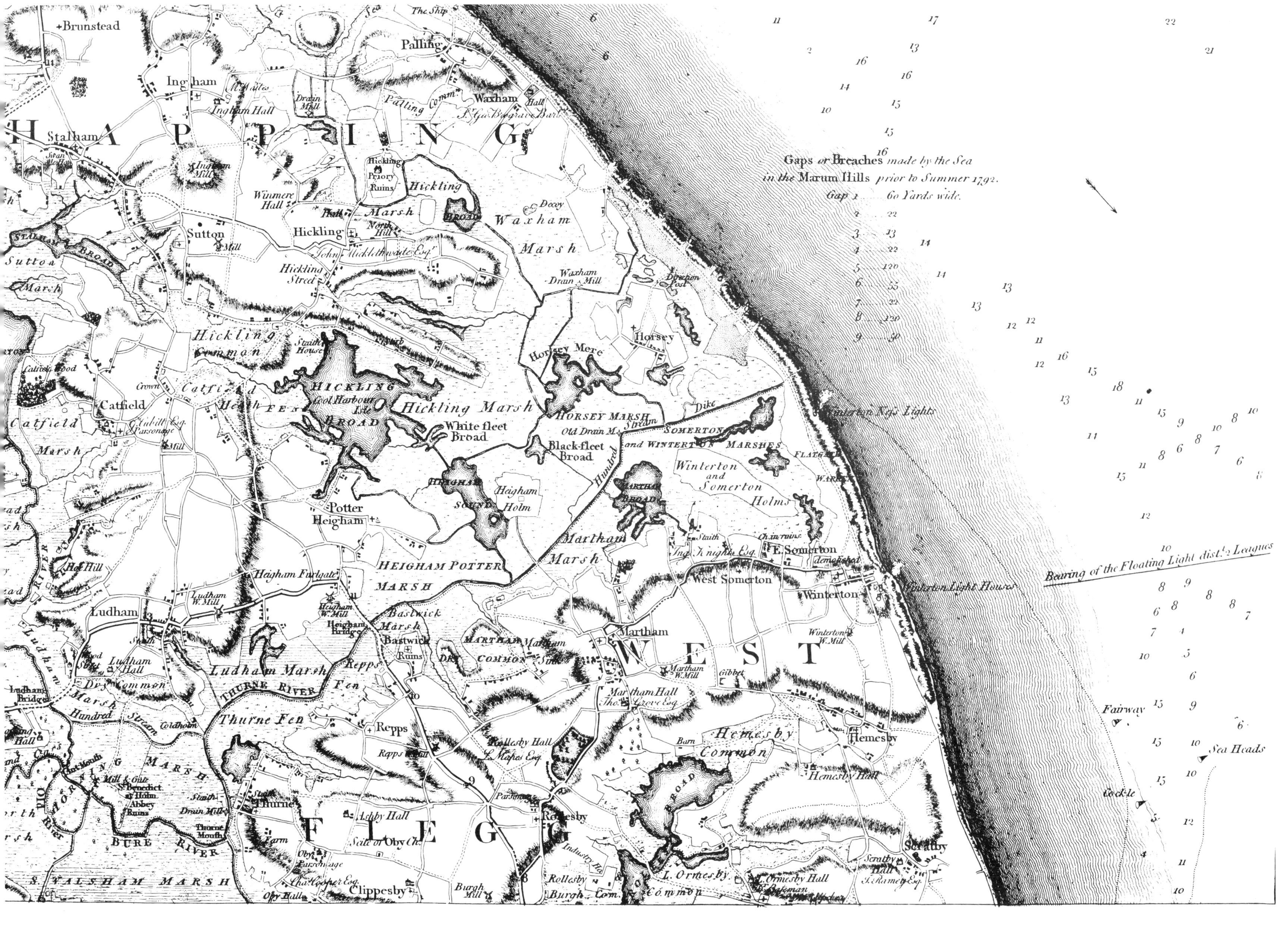

Brunstead
The Ship
Palling
Ingham
Ingham Hall
Waxham
Palling Comm.
H A P P I N G
Stalham
Hickling Priory Ruins
Hickling
Winmere Hall
Sutton
Hickling
Waxham Marsh
Sutton Broad
Hickling Street
Waxham Drain Mill
Horsey
Hickling Common
Horsey Mere
Catfield
Hickling Broad
Hickling Marsh
White fleet Broad
Horsey Marsh
Black-fleet Broad
Somerton and Winterton Marshes
Winterton and Somerton Holms
Marsh
Potter Heigham
Heigham Holm
Heigham Sound
Martham Broad
Martham Marsh
E. Somerton
West Somerton
Winterton
Heigham Potter Marsh
Heigham Furlgate
Ludham
Bastwick Marsh
Bastwick
Martham
W E S T
Ludham Hall
Ludham Marsh
Thurne River
Repps Fen
Martham Common
Martham Hall
Thurne Fen
Repps
Hemesby Common
Hemesby
Hemesby Hall
Rollesby Hall
Ludham Bridge
Horning Marsh
St. Benedict at Holm Abbey Ruins
Thurne
Thurne Mouth
Ashby Hall
F L E G G
Rollesby
Bure River
Scratby
Scratby Hall
L. Ormesby Common
L. Ormesby Hall
S. Walsham Marsh
Clippesby
Oby Hall
Burgh Mill
Rollesby Burgh Com.
Gaps or Breaches made by the Sea in the Marum Hills prior to Summer 1792.
Gap 1 ..... 60 Yards wide.
Winterton Ness Lights
Winterton Light House
Bearing of the Floating Light dist. 2 Leagues
Fairway
Sea Heads
Cockle

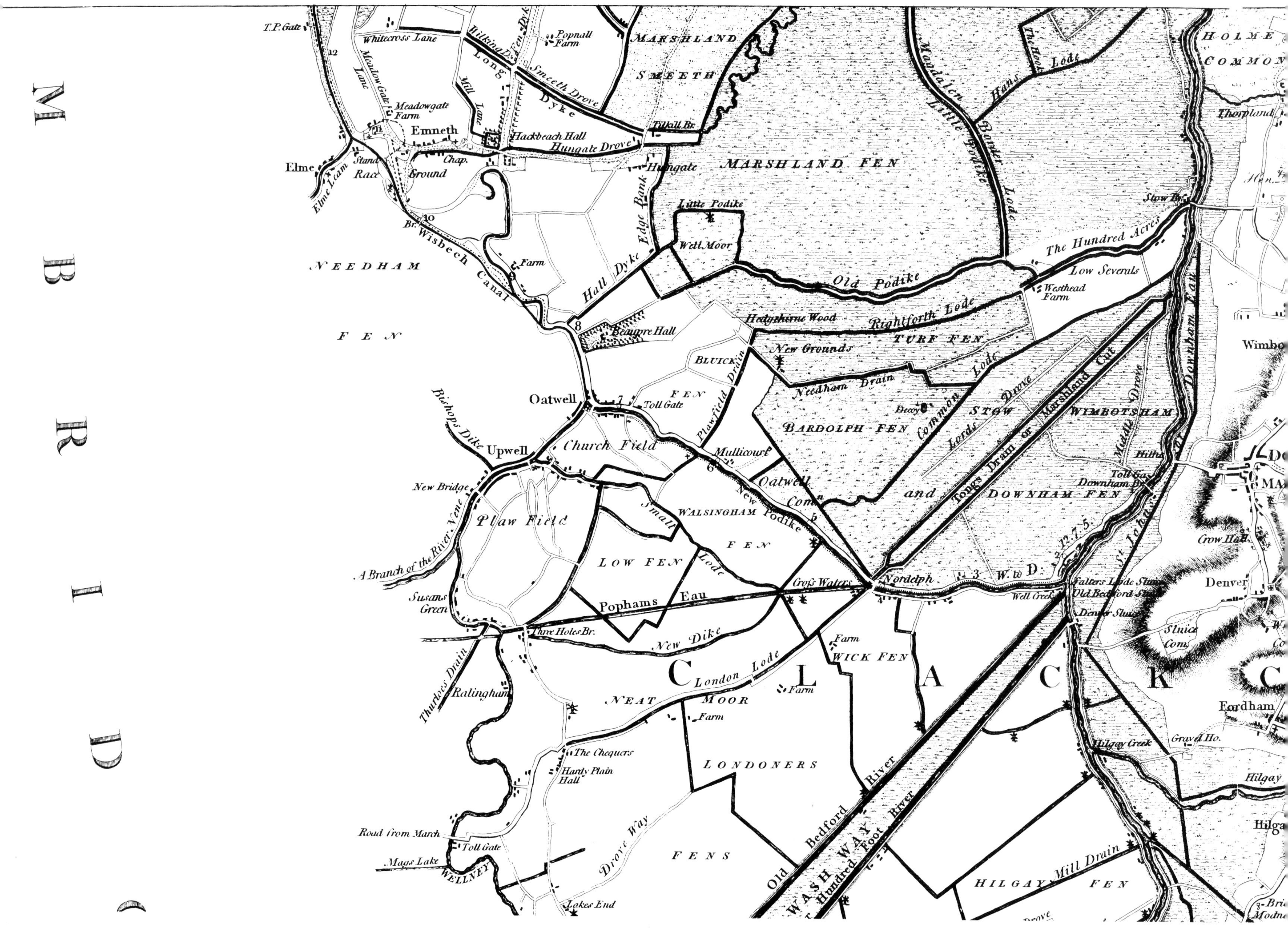
MARSHLAND
SMEETH
MARSHLAND FEN
HOLME COMMON
NEEDHAM FEN
TURF FEN
BLUICK FEN
BARDOLPH FEN
STOW
WIMBOTSHAM
DOWNHAM FEN
WALSINGHAM FEN
LOW FEN
WICK FEN
NEAT MOOR
LONDONERS
FENS
HILGAY FEN
Emneth
Elme
Oatwell
Upwell
Denver
Fordham
Hilgay
Whitecross Lane
Popnall Farm
Meadowgate Farm
Hackbeach Hall
Hungate Drove
Tilkill Br.
Little Podike
Well Moor
Old Podike
Hedgehirne Wood
Rightforth Lode
New Grounds
Needham Drain
Beaupre Hall
Church Field
Plaw Field
Pophams Eau
Three Holes Br.
New Dike
London Lode
Old Bedford River
Hundred Foot River
Hilgay Mill Drain
Downham Eau
Wisbech Canal
The Hundred Acres
Low Severals
Westhead Farm
Tongs Drain or Marshland Cut
Toll Gate
Nordelph
Gross Waters
Thurloes Drain
Ralingham
The Chequers
Hardy Plain Hall
Road from March
Mags Lake
WELLNEY
Lokes End
Drove Way
New Bridge
Susans Green
A Branch of the River Nene
Bishops Dike
Mullicourt
Stow Br.
Thorpland
Downham Br.
Salters Lode Sluice
Old Bedford Sluice
Denver Sluice
Sluice Com.
Crow Hall
Gravel Ho.
Hilgay Creek
M B R I D
C L A C K C

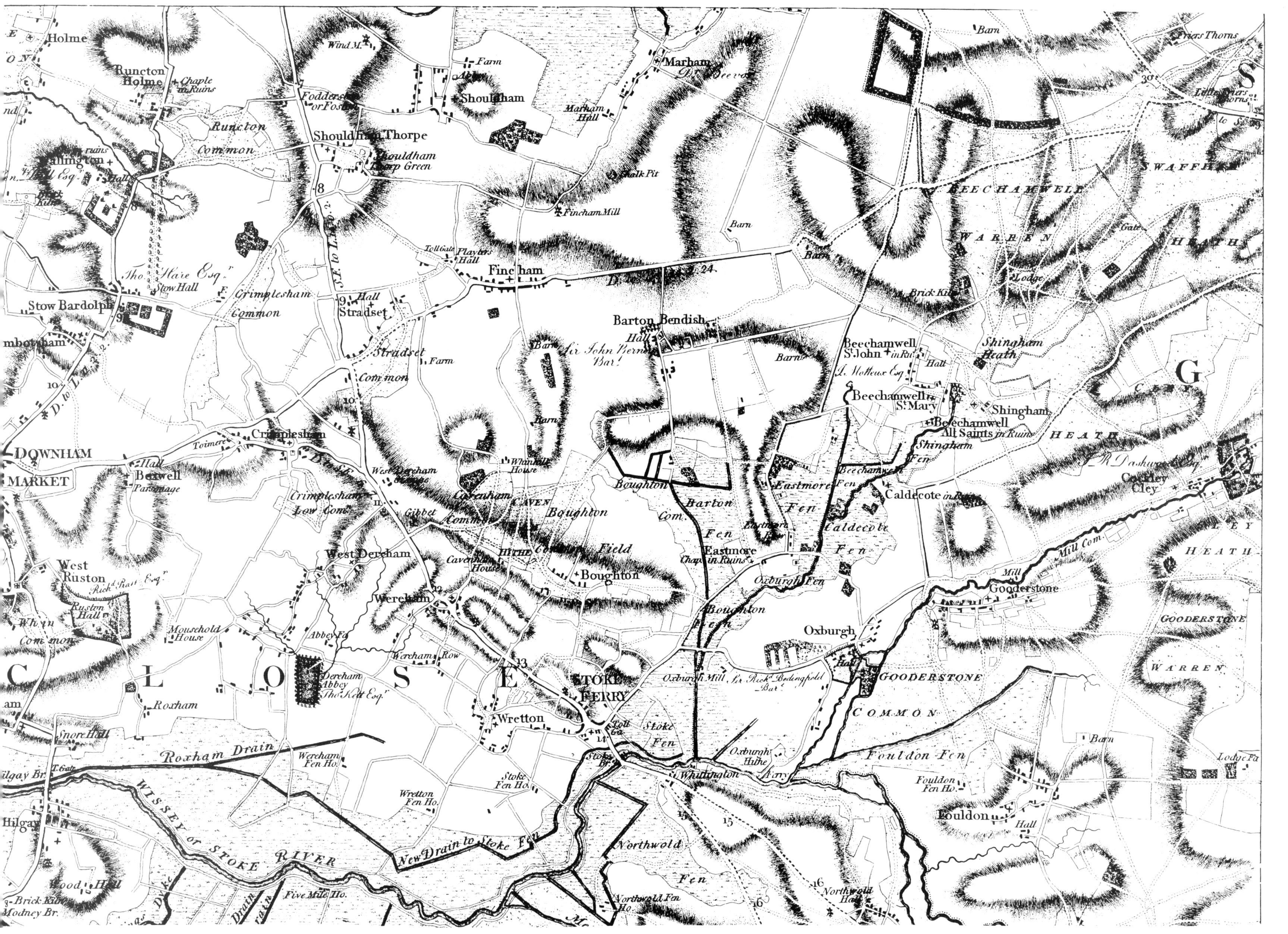

Holme
Runcton Holme
Chaple in Ruins
Wind M.
Farm
Abbey
Shouldham
Marham
Marham Hall
Barn
Friars Thorns
Fodderston or Foston
Runcton Common
Shouldham Thorpe
Shouldham Thorp Green
Chalk Pit
Fincham Mill
Barn
Beechamwell Warren
Swaffham
Heath
Stow Hall
Stow Bardolph
Crimplesham Common
Hall
Stradset
Toll Gate
Playters Hall
Fincham
Barn
Lodge
Brick Kiln
Barton Bendish
Hall
Stradset Common
Farm
Barn
Beechamwell St. John in Ruins
Hall
Shingham Heath
Beechamwell St. Mary
Shingham
Beechamwell All Saints in Ruins
Shingham Fen
Heath
DOWNHAM MARKET
Bexwell Parsonage
Crimplesham
Toimere
Whinhill House
West Dereham Commons
Crimplesham Low Com.
Gibbet
Cavenham
Boughton Com.
Barton Fen
Eastmore Fen
Caldecote Fen
Beechamwell Fen
Caldecote in Ruins
Boughton Field
Eastmore Chap. in Ruins
West Ruston
Ruston Hall
West Dereham
Cavenham House
Boughton
Oxburgh Fen
Mill Com.
Mill
Gooderstone
Werham
Mousehold House
Abbey Fa.
Boughton Fen
Oxburgh
Gooderstone
Warren
Whin Common
C L O S E
Dereham Abbey Tho. Kett Esq.
Roxham
Wereham Row
STOKE FERRY
Oxburgh Mill
GOODERSTONE COMMON
Wretton
Toll Ga.
Stoke Fen
Snore Hall
Roxham Drain
Wereham Fen Ho.
Stoke Br.
Oxburgh Hithe
Whittington Ferry
Foulden Fen
Barn
Lodge Fa.
Stoke Fen Ho.
Wretton Fen Ho.
Foulden Fen Ho.
Foulden
Hall
Hilgay
WISSEY or STOKE RIVER
New Drain to Stoke Fen
Northwold
Northwold Fen
Five Mile Ho.
Northwold Fen Ho.
Northwold Hall
Wood Hall
Brick Kiln
Modney Br.
Drain

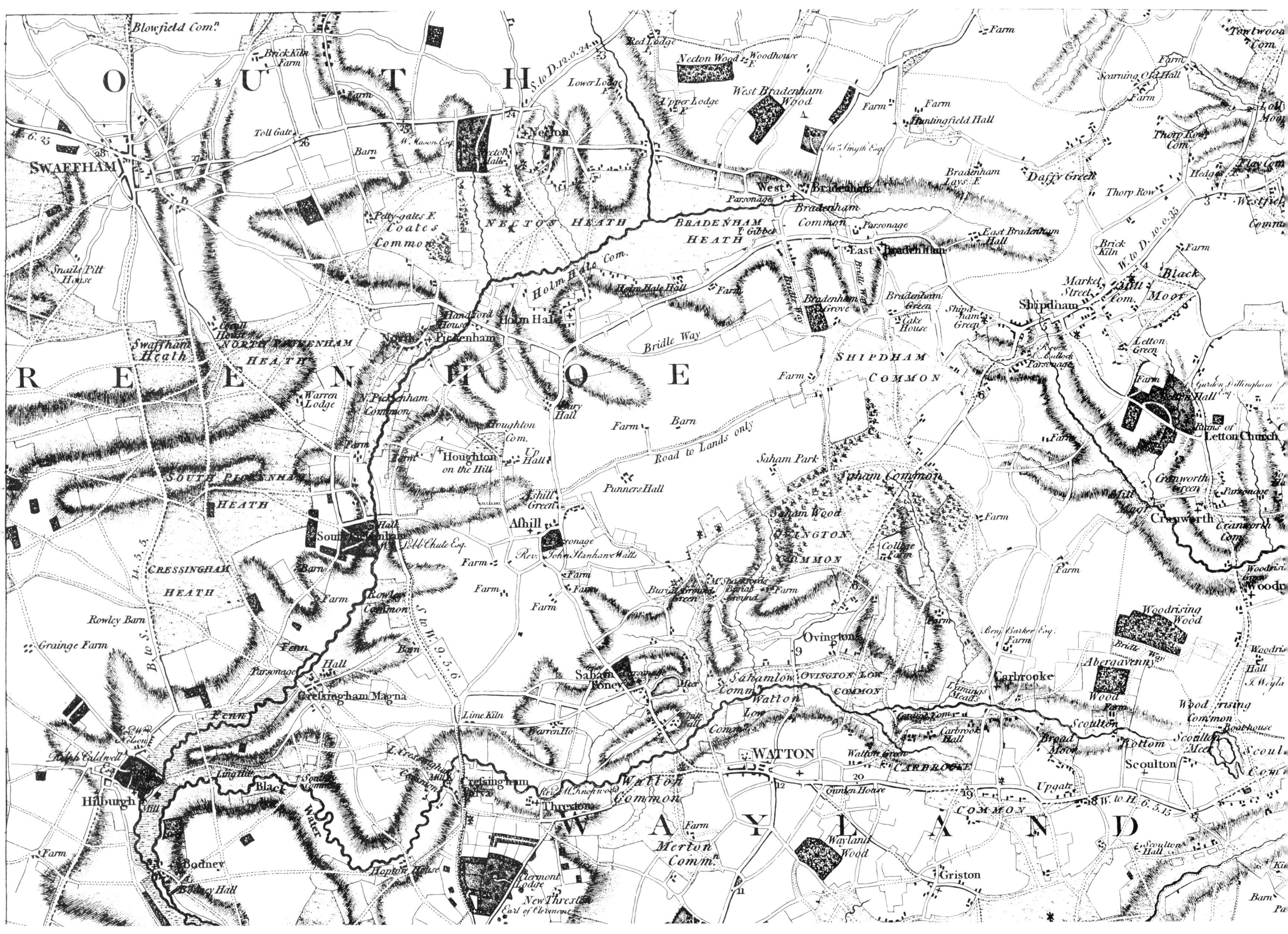

Blowfield Comn.
Brick Kiln Farm
SOUTH
GREENHOE
WAYLAND
SWAFFHAM
Toll Gate
Barn
Necton
Necton Hall
W. Mason Esq.
S. to D. 12. 0. 24
Red Lodge F.
Lower Lodge F.
Necton Wood
Woodhouse F.
West Bradenham Wood
Upper Lodge F.
Jas. Smyth Esq.
Farm
Huntingfield Hall
Scarning Old Hall
Tortwood Com.
Thorp Row Com.
Daffy Green
Thorp Row
Bradenham Lays F.
West
Bradenham
Parsonage
Bradenham Common
NECTON HEATH
BRADENHAM HEATH
T. Gibbet
East Bradenham
East Bradenham Hall
W. to D. 10. 0. 35
Brick Kiln
Black Moor
Mill Com.
Market Street
Shipdham
Petty-gates F.
Coates Common
Snails Pitt House
Holm Hale Com.
Holm Hale Hall
Holm Hale
Bradenham Grove
Bradenham Green
Cake House
Shipdham Green
Bridle Way
Handford House
North Pickenham
Swaffham Heath
NORTH PICKENHAM HEATH
SHIPDHAM COMMON
Letton Green
Rev. C. Bullock Parsonage
Warren Lodge
N. Pickenham Common
Bury Hall
Farm
Barn
Letton Hall
Ruins of Letton Church
Houghton Com.
Houghton on the Hill
Up Hall
Road to Lands only
Saham Park
Saham Common
Cranworth Green
Parsonage
SOUTH PICKENHAM HEATH
Punners Hall
Ashill Green
Ashill
Saham Wood
OVINGTON COMMON
Cranworth
Cranworth Com.
South Pickenham
Hall
Lobb Chute Esq.
Parsonage
Rev. John Stanh(«ope) Watts
College Farm
CRESSINGHAM HEATH
Rowley Common
S. to W. 9. 5. 6
Burial Ground Green
Mr. Shackford's Burial Ground
Woodrising
Rowley Barn
Grainge Farm
B. to S.
14. 5. 5
Fenn
Hall
Parsonage
Ovington
Benj. Barker Esq. Farm
Woodrising Wood
Bridle Way
Saham Toney
Saham Low Comm.
OVINGTON LOW COMMON
Watton Low Comm.
Carbrooke
Abergavenny Wood
Lamings Meals
Cressingham Magna
Lime Kiln
Warren Ho.
Carbrook Hall
Broad Moor
Scoulton
Bottom
Scoulton Meer
Scoulton Com.
Wood rising Common
Boat house
Ralph Caldwell Esq.
Hilburgh
Mill
Black Water
Ling Hill
Cressingham Parva
Threxton
Rev. Mr. Knopwood
Watton Common
WATTON
Watton Green
CARBROOKE
Garden House
COMMON
Upgate
W. to H. 6. 5. 15
Scoulton Hall
Bodney
Bodney Hall
Hopton House
Clermont Lodge
New Threxton
Earl of Clermont
Merton Comm.
Wayland Wood
Griston
Barn

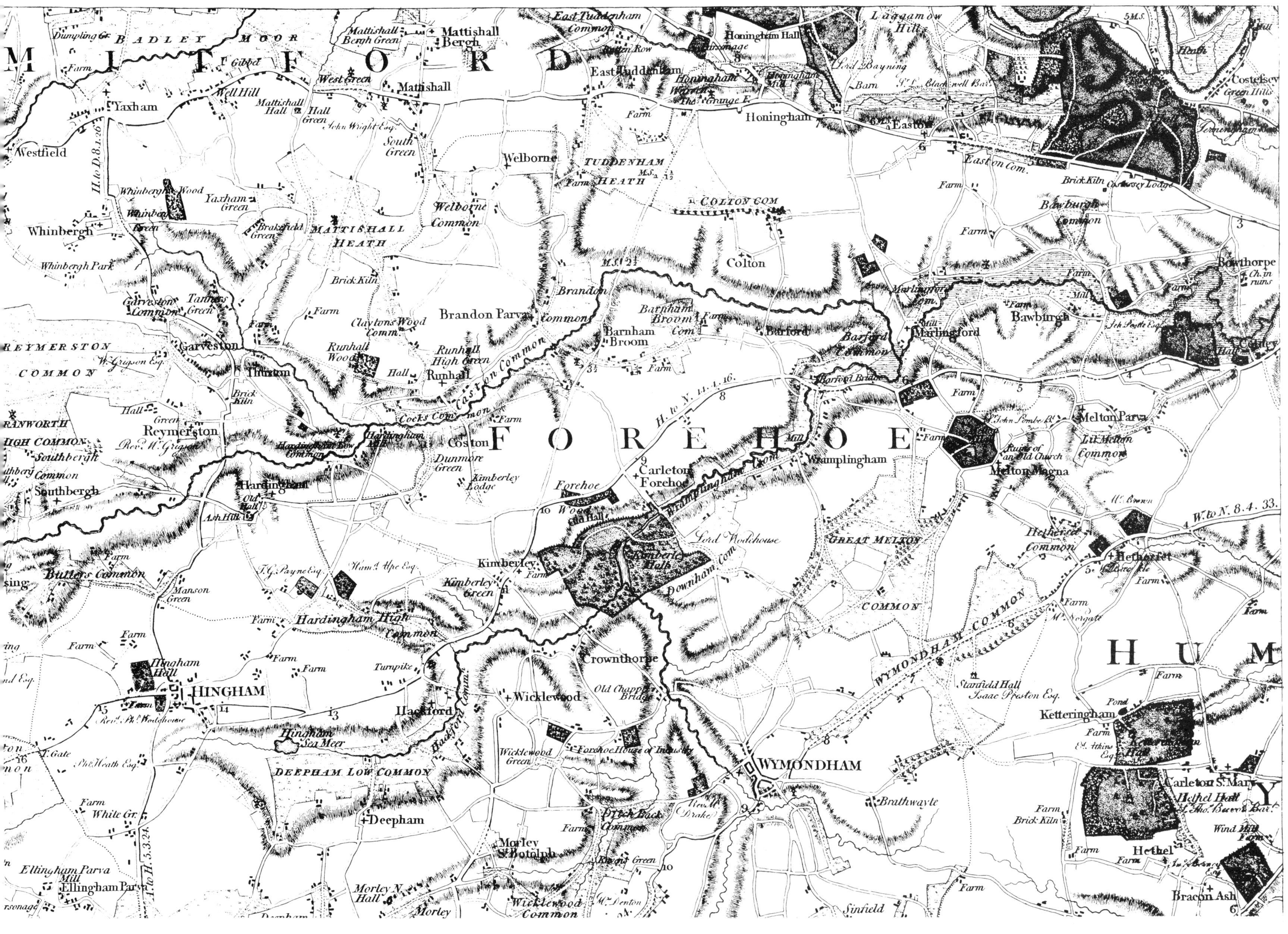

M I T F O R D
F O R E H O E
H U M
BADLEY MOOR
Dumpling Gr.
Farm
Gibbet
Yaxham
Westfield
Well Hill
Mattishall Hall
Hall Green
John Wright Esq.
West Green
Mattishall
Mattishall Bergh Green
Mattishall Bergh
South Green
East Tuddenham Common
East Tuddenham
Honingham Hall
Honingham
Honingham Mill
The Grange F.
Easton
Easton Com.
Laggamow Hill
Lord Bayning
Barn
Costessey
Green Hills
Heath
Brick Kiln
Costessey Lodge
Welborne
Welborne Common
TUDDENHAM HEATH
COLTON COM
Colton
Bawburgh Common
Bawburgh
Bowthorpe
Ch. in ruins
Whinbergh Wood
Whinbergh Green
Whinbergh
Whinbergh Park
Yaxham Green
Brakefield Green
MATTISHALL HEATH
Brick Kiln
Farm
Claytons Wood Comm.
Brandon Parva
Brandon Common
Barnham Broom Com.
Barnham Broom
Barford
Barford Common
Barford Bridge
Marlingford Com.
Marlingford
Mill
Garveston Common
Tanners Green
Garveston
REYMERSTON COMMON
W. Grigson Esq.
Thurston
Runhall Wood
Runhall High Green
Runhall
Hall
Caston Common
Cocks Common
Brick Kiln
Reymerston
RANWORTH HIGH COMMON
Rev. Mr. Grigson
Southbergh Common
Southbergh
Hardingham
Hardingham Low Common
Old Hall
Ash Hill
Coston
Dunmore Green
Kimberley Lodge
Forehoe
Forehoe Wood
Carleton Forehoe
H. to N. 14. 4. 16.
Wramplingham
Wramplingham Com.
Farm
Melton Parva
Lit. Melton Common
Ruins of an Old Church
Melton Magna
Mr. Brown
W. to N. 8. 4. 33.
Hethersett Common
Hethersett
GREAT MELTON
COMMON
Lord Wodehouse
Kimberley Hall
Downham Com.
Kimberley
Kimberley Green
Butters Common
Manson Green
T. G. Payne Esq.
Ham. Alpe Esq.
Hardingham High Common
WYMONDHAM COMMON
Mr. Norgate
Farm
Turnpike
Crownthorpe
Old Chappel Bridge
Hingham Hall
HINGHAM
Rev. Phil. Wodehouse
Hackford
Hackford Comm.
Wicklewood
Staufield Hall
Isaac Preston Esq.
Ketteringham
Pond
Hingham Sea Meer
Phil. Heath Esq.
T. Gate
DEEPHAM LOW COMMON
Wicklewood Green
Forehoe House of Industry
WYMONDHAM
Carleton S. Mary
Hethel Hall
Brathwayte
Farm
Brick Kiln
White Gr.
Deepham
Ditch Back Common
Rev. Mr. Drake
Morley St. Botolph
Kings Green
Hethel
Wind Mill
Ellingham Parva
Mill
Morley N. Hall
Wicklewood Common
Mr. Denton
Morley
Sinfield
Bracon Ash
H. to H. 5. 3. 24.

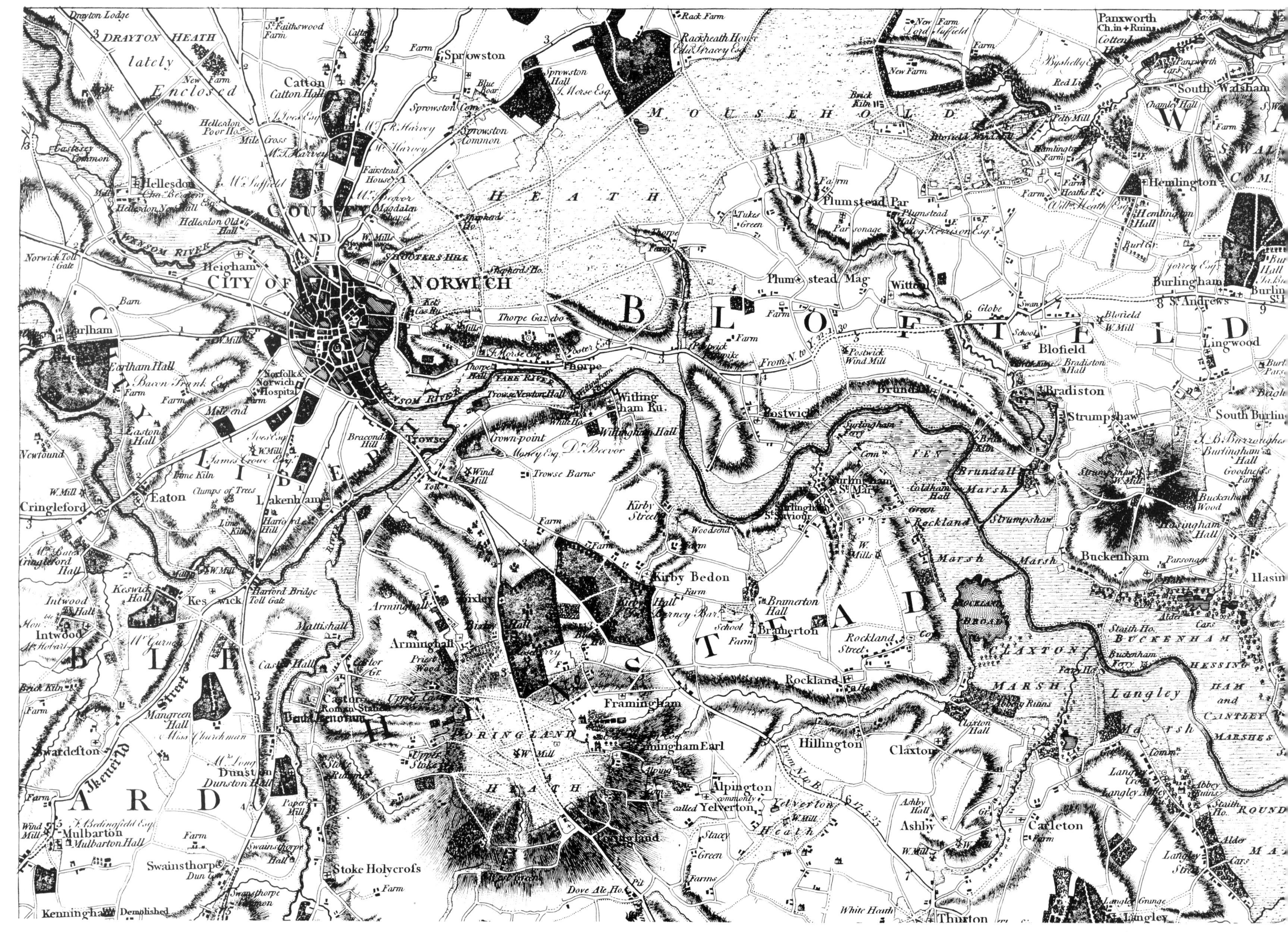

Drayton Lodge
DRAYTON HEATH
lately
Enclosed
St. Faithswood Farm
Sprowston
Catton
Catton Hall
Sprowston Hall
J. Morse Esq.
Rack Farm
Rackheath House
Sprowston Com.
Sprowston Common
Blue Boar
M O U S E H O L D
H E A T H
Panxworth
South Walsham
New Farm
Red Lo.
Petty Mill
Blofield Wind Mill
Hemlington
Hemlington Hall
Hellesdon
Hellesdon Poor Ho.
Hellesdon Old Hall
Mile Cross
Costessey Common
WENSOM RIVER
COUNTY
AND
CITY OF
NORWICH
Heigham
Norwich Toll Gate
Earlham
Earlham Hall
Bacon Frank Esq.
Norfolk & Norwich Hospital
Mile end
Shooters Hill
Magdalen Chapel
Fairstead House
Thorpe Gazebo
Thorpe
YARE RIVER
Trowse Newton Hall
Witlingham Ru.
Witlingham Hall
Crown point
Dr. Beever
Trowse
Trowse Barns
Bracondale Hill
Eaton
Cringleford
Newfound
Lakenham
Harford Hill
Clumps of Trees
Lime Kiln
B L O F I E L D
Plumstead Par
Plumstead Mag
Plumstead Hall
Parsonage
Tukes Green
Witton
Postwick
Postwick Wind Mill
From N. to Y.
Globe
Swan
Blofield
Bradiston
Bradiston Hall
Lingwood
Burlingham
St. Andrews
Strumpshaw
Strumpshaw W. Mill
South Burlingham
Burlingham Hall
Brundall
Brundall Marsh
Surlingham
St. Mary
St. Saviour
Surlingham Ferry
FEN
Coldham Hall
Rockland Marsh
Rockland Broad
Rockland Street
Rockland
Kirby Street
Kirby Bedon
Kirby Hall
Woodsend
Bramerton
Bramerton Hall
School Farm
Buckenham
Buckenham Wood
Hasingham Hall
Parsonage
Staith Ho.
BUCKENHAM
Buckenham Ferry
CLAXTON
MARSH
Claxton
Claxton Hall
Langley
Marsh
HESSINGHAM and CANTLEY MARSHES
Harford Bridge Toll Gate
Keswick
Keswick Hall
Intwood
Intwood Hall
Mr. Bates Cringleford Hall
Arminghall
Mattishall
Bixley
Caister Hall
Castor Roman Station
Upper Stoke
Stoke Ruins
Poringland
P O R I N G L A N D
H E A T H
Framingham
Framingham Earl
Hillington
Alpington
Yelverton
Yelverton Heath
Ashby
Ashby Hall
Carleton
Langley Abbey
Abbey Ruins
Langley Street
Alder Cars
Swardeston
Mangreen Hall
Miss Churchman
Dunston
Dunston Hall
Paper Mill
Brick Kiln
A R D
Mulbarton
Mulbarton Hall
J. Bedingfield Esq.
Swainsthorpe
Swainsthorpe Hall
Stoke Holycrofs
Kenningham Demolished
Dove Ale Ho.
Stacey Green
Farms
White Heath
Thurton
Langley Grange
Jkenield Street

Great Ormesby
L. Ormesby
Ormesby Old Ch. in Ruins
Burgh St. Mary in Ruins
Burgh St. Marg.
Billockby
Kings Arms
Upton Broad
Upton
Upton Green
Fishley
Fishley Hall
Clipesbey Marshes
Billockby Marsh
Obey
Obey and Drain Mill
EAST
Filby
Filby Common
Nova Scotia
Thrigby
Thrigby Hall
Mautby
Carpenters F.
Castor
Castor Old Hall
West Castor in Ruins
Flour Wind Mill
FLEGG
Com.n Field
Runham
Runham Hall
Stokesby
Stokesby Green
Stokesby Marsh
Muck Fleet
Wey Bridge
Acle
Hermitage
Dangate
Ferry
Herringby Demolished
Rising F.
Castor Marsh
Runham & Mautby Marshes
ACLE WET COMMON
Drain W. Mill
Seven Mile House
Six Mile House
Five Mile House
Four Mile Ho.
Three Mile House
Two Mile Ho.
Bure River
Gibbet
Yarmouth
Fort
Denes
Acle Tunstall
Acle Marsh Ho.
Tunstall
Tunstall Low Farm
Halvergate
Lock Gate Marsh Ho.
Breydon Water
West Town
YARMOUTH
S HAM
Halvergate Marsh Ho.
Wickhampton
Marshes
Moulton
Beighton
Freethorpe
Southwood
Southwood Hall
Cantley
Limpenhoe
Brick Kiln
Reedham Cars
Reedham Hall
Reedham
Reedham Ferry
Drain W. Mills
Lower Seven Mile Ho
Upper Seven Mile Ho. & Mill
Five Mile Ho.
Six Mile Ho.
Burgh Flat
Yare River
Ravenningham
Southwood and Limpenhoe Marshes
South Town
The Denes
Ware House
Battery
Jetty
Ferry
Burgh Castle
Garrianonum
Gorleston
Bradwell
Belton Common
Belton
Belton Hall
Lothing
Yarmouth Roads
Cockle
Scroby
St. Nicholas
St. Nicholas Gatt
Corton

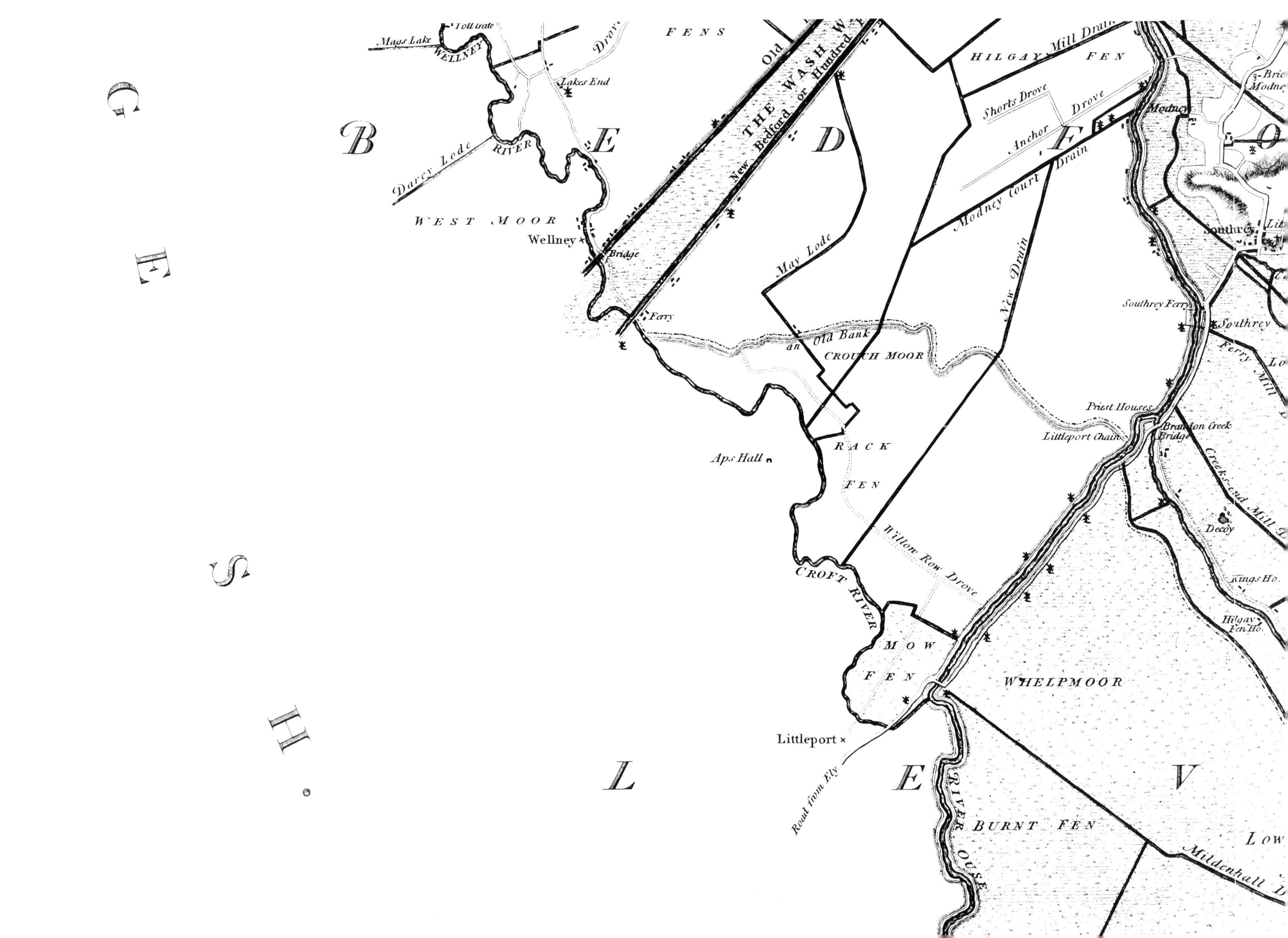

Toll Gate
Mags Lake
WELLNEY
FENS
Old
THE WASH W
New Bedford or Hundred
HILGAY Mill Drain
FEN
Lakes End
Shorts Drove
Anchor Drove
Modney
Modney Court Drain
B
E
D
F
O
Darcy Lode
RIVER
WEST MOOR
Wellney
Bridge
May Lode
New Drain
Southrey
Southrey Ferry
Southrey
Ferry
Ferry Mill
an Old Bank
CROUCH MOOR
Priest Houses
Brandon Creek Bridge
Littleport Chain
Creeks-end Mill
RACK
FEN
Aps Hall
Decoy
Willow Row Drove
Kings Ho.
CROFT RIVER
Hilgay Fen Ho.
MOW
FEN
WHELPMOOR
Littleport
Road from Ely
G
E
S
H
L
E
V
RIVER OUSE
BURNT FEN
Low
Mildenhall

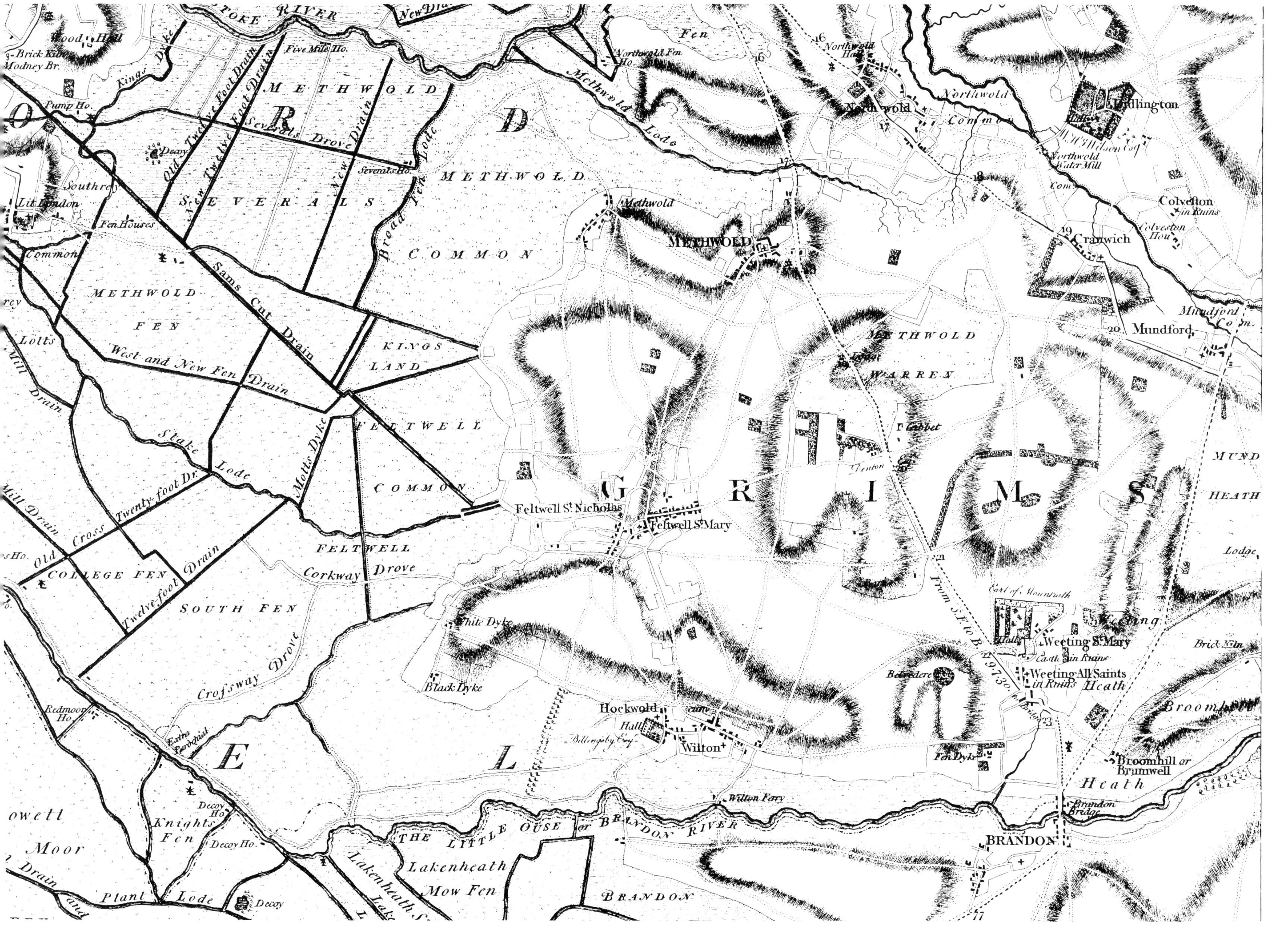

Wood Hall
Brick Kiln
Modney Br.
Pump Ho.
Kings Dyke
Five Mile Ho.
Old Twelve Foot Drain
New Twelve Foot Drain
METHWOLD
SEVERALS
Severals Drove
New Drain
Severals Ho.
Broad Fen Lode
Decoy
Southrey
Lit. London
Fen Houses
Common
METHWOLD
COMMON
Methwold Lode
Northwold Fen Ho.
Fen
Northwold Hall
Northwold
Northwold Common
Didlington Hall
W. H. Wilson Esq.
Northwold Water Mill
Colveston in Ruins
Colveston Hou.
Cranwich
Mundford
Mundford Com.
Methwold
METHWOLD
Sams Cut Drain
METHWOLD FEN
West and New Fen Drain
KINGS LAND
FELTWELL
COMMON
Stake Lode
Motts Dyke
Mill Drain
Old Cross Twenty-foot Dr.
COLLEGE FEN
Twelve-foot Drain
SOUTH FEN
FELTWELL
Corkway Drove
Crossway Drove
METHWOLD WARREN
Lodge
Gibbet
Denton
GRIMS
Feltwell St. Nicholas
Feltwell St. Mary
From S. Flo B.
Earl of Mountrath
Weeting
Weeting St. Mary
Hall
Castle in Ruins
Weeting All Saints in Ruins
Heath
Belvedere
White Dyke
Black Dyke
Hockwold Hall
Billingsby Esq.
Wilton
Fen Dyke
MUND HEATH
Lodge
Brick Kiln
Broomhill
Broomhill or Brumwell
Heath
Brandon Bridge
BRANDON
Wilton Fery
THE LITTLE OUSE or BRANDON RIVER
Redmoor Ho.
Extra Parochial
Decoy Ho.
Knights Fen
Decoy Ho.
Moor
Plant Lode
Decoy
Lakenheath Mow Fen
BRANDON
E
L

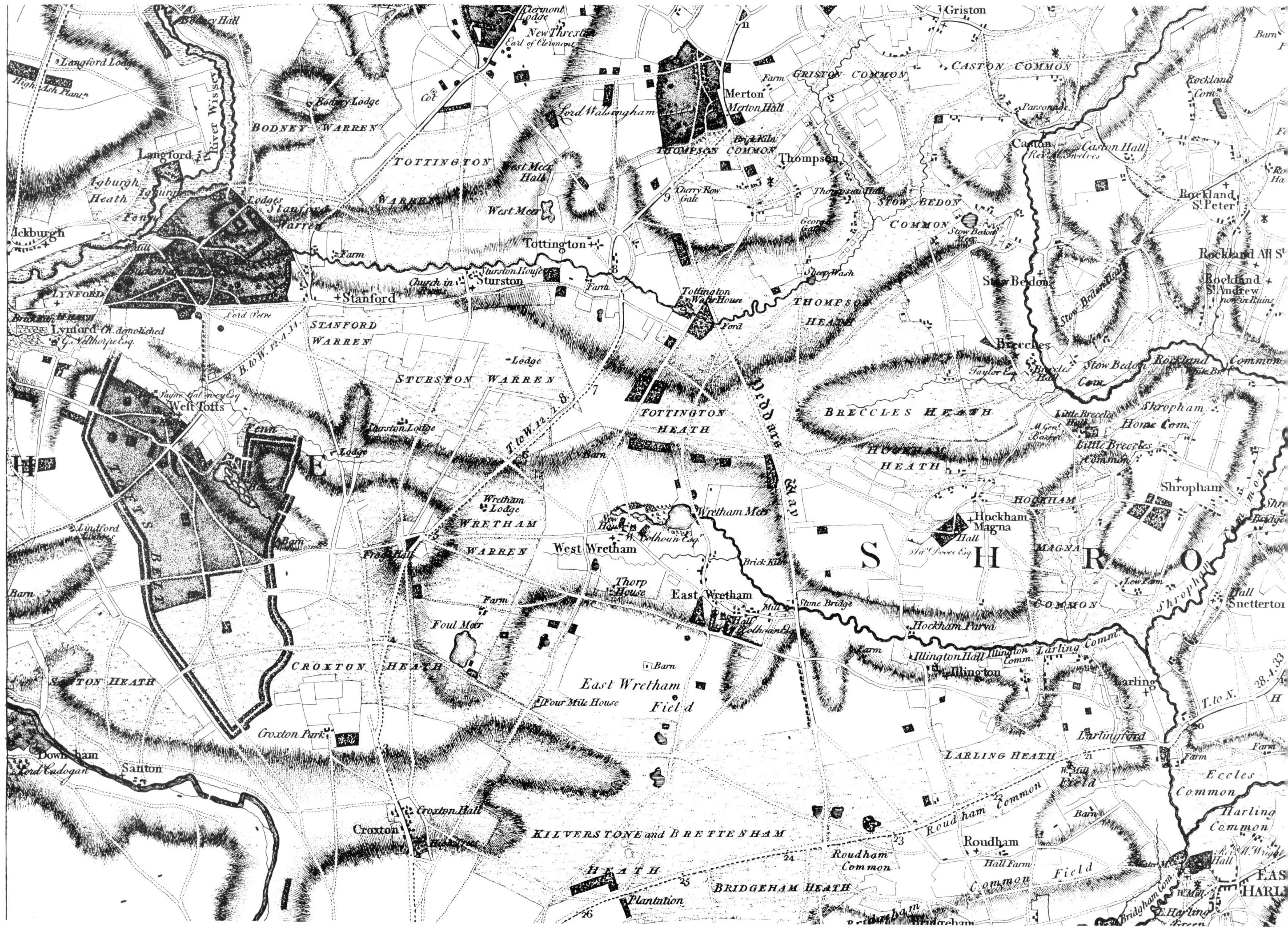

Clermont Lodge
New Threxton
Earl of Clermont
Griston
Langford Lodge
High Ash Plantn
Bodney Lodge
BODNEY WARREN
River Wissey
Langford
Igburgh Heath
Ickburgh
Lodges
Stanford Warren
TOTTINGTON WARREN
West Meer Hall
West Meer
Lord Walsingham
Merton
Merton Hall
Farm
GRISTON COMMON
CASTON COMMON
Rockland Com.
Parsonage
Brick Kiln
THOMPSON COMMON
Thompson
Cherry Row Gate
Thompson Hall
STOW BEDON COMMON
Stow Bedon Meer
Caston
Caston Hall
Rockland St. Peter
Rockland All St.
Rockland St. Andrew now in Ruins
Tottington
Farm
Sturston House
Church in Ruins
Sturston
Stanford
LYNFORD
Lord Petre
Lynford Ch. demolished
Sheep Wash
Tottington Water House
Ford
THOMPSON HEATH
Stow Bedon
Stow Bedon Heath
STANFORD WARREN
Lodge
STURSTON WARREN
Breccles
Breccles Hall
Stow Bedon Com.
Rockland Common
Taylor Esq.
West Tofts
Sturston Lodge
TOTTINGTON HEATH
BRECCLES HEATH
Little Breccles Hall
Shropham Home Com.
Little Breccles Common
Lodge
Barn
HOCKHAM HEATH
Wretham Lodge
WRETHAM WARREN
Wretham Meer
Hockham Magna
Hall
HOCKHAM MAGNA
Shropham
Lindford Lodges
Barn
West Wretham
Brick Kiln
S H R O
Thorp House
East Wretham
Stone Bridge
Mill
Hall
COMMON
Low Farm
Hall
Snetterton
Foul Meer
Farm
Hockham Parva
Illington Hall
Illington Comm.
Illington
Larling Comm.
CROXTON HEATH
SANTON HEATH
Barn
East Wretham Field
Four Mile House
Larling
T. to N.
Croxton Park
Downham
Lord Cadogan
Santon
Larlingford
LARLING HEATH
Farm
Eccles Common
W. Mill Field
Roudham Common
Harling Common
Croxton Hall
Croxton
KILVERSTONE and BRETTENHAM HEATH
Roudham
Roudham Common
Hall Farm
Common Field
Barn
BRIDGEHAM HEATH
Plantation
Bridgham Com.
E. Harling
W. Mill
EAST HARLING

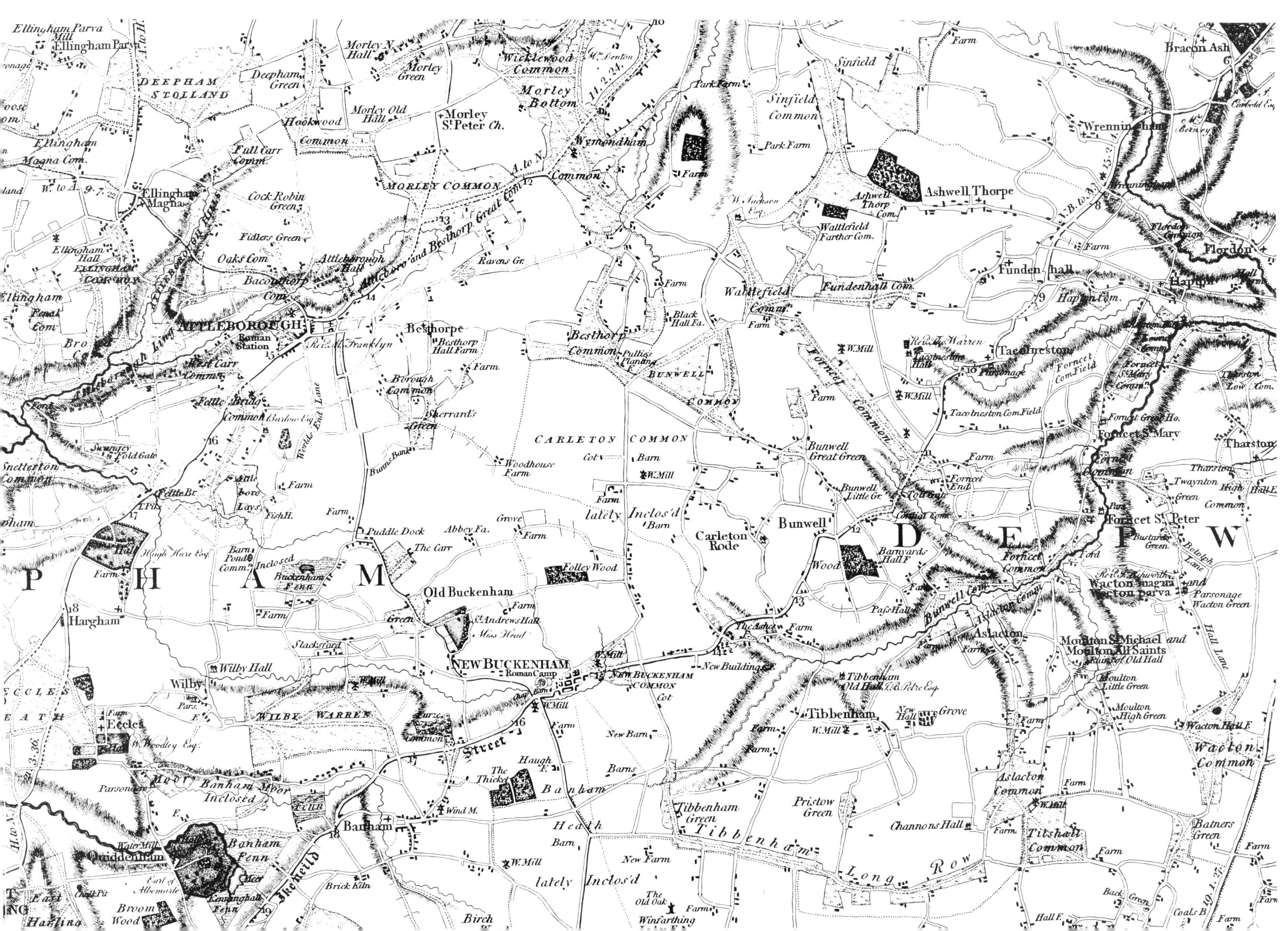

Ellingham Parva
Mill
Ellingham Parva
DEEPHAM
STOLLAND
Deepham Green
Morley N. Hall
Morley Green
Wicklewood Common
Morley Bottom
Morley Old Hall
Morley St. Peter Ch.
Hookwood Common
Ellingham Magna Com.
Full Carr Comm.
Wymondham
Common
MORLEY COMMON
Ellingham Magna
Cock Robin Green
Fidlers Green
Oaks Com
Attleborough Hall
Attleboro and Besthorp Great Com.
Ravens Gr.
Ellingham Hall
Bacouthorp Com
ATTLEBOROUGH
Roman Station
Besthorpe
Besthorp Hall Farm
Besthorp Common
Pulliss Planting
BUNWELL COMMON
Park Farm
Sinfield
Sinfield Common
Park Farm
Ashwell Thorpe
Ashwell Thorp Com.
Wattlefield Farther Com.
Wattlefield Comm.
Fundenhall Com.
Funden hall
Black Hall Fa.
Forncet Common
Tacolneston
Tacolneston Hall
Parsonage
Tacolneston Com Field
Forncet Com Field
Forncet St. Mary
Bracon Ash
Wrenningham
Flordon
Hapton
Hapton Com.
Tharston
Tharston Low Com.
West Carr Comm.
Borough Common
Sherrard's Green
Kettle Bridg Common
Barlow Esq.
Worlds End Lane
Snetterton Common
Kettle Br.
Fold Gate
Farm
Fish H.
Puddle Dock
Abbey Fa.
Grove
The Carr
Woodhouse Farm
CARLETON COMMON
Barn
W. Mill
lately Inclos'd
Bunwell Great Green
Bunwell Little Gr.
Bunwell
Carleton Rode
Wood
Barnyards Hall F.
Forncet End
Forncet St. Peter
Forncet Common
Twaynton Green
Tharston High Common
Bustards Green
Botolph Lane
Wacton magna and Wacton parva
Parsonage
Wacton Green
D E P W
P H A M
Hall
Hugh Hare Esq.
Farm
Barn Pond Comm.
Inclosed
Buckenham Fenn
Folley Wood
Old Buckenham
St. Andrews Hall
Miss Head
Green
Hargham
Slacksford
Wilby Hall
Wilby
NEW BUCKENHAM
Roman Camp
NEW BUCKENHAM COMMON
New Buildings
The Ash
Pass Hall
Bunwell Com.
Aslacton Comm.
Aslacton
Moulton St. Michael and Moulton All Saints
Ruins of Old Hall
Moulton Little Green
Moulton High Green
Wacton Hall F.
Wacton Common
Hall Lane
Tibbenham Old Hall
I. B. Petre Esq.
Tibbenham
New Hall
Grove
ECCLES HEATH
Eccles
W. Woodley Esq.
WILBY WARREN
Furze Common
Street
Haugh F.
The Thicket
Banham
New Barn
Barns
Aslacton Common
Parsonage
Banham Moor Inclosed
Fenn
Wind M.
Banham
Heath
Barn
Tibbenham Green
Tibbenham Long Row
Pristow Green
Channons Hall
Titshall Common
Batners Green
Water Mill
Quiddenham
Banham Fenn
Ikenild
Brick Kiln
W. Mill
lately Inclos'd
New Farm
The Old Oak
Winfarthing
Earl of Albemarle
Kenninghall Fenn
Broom Wood
East Harling
Birch
Back Green
Coals B
Hall F.
Farm

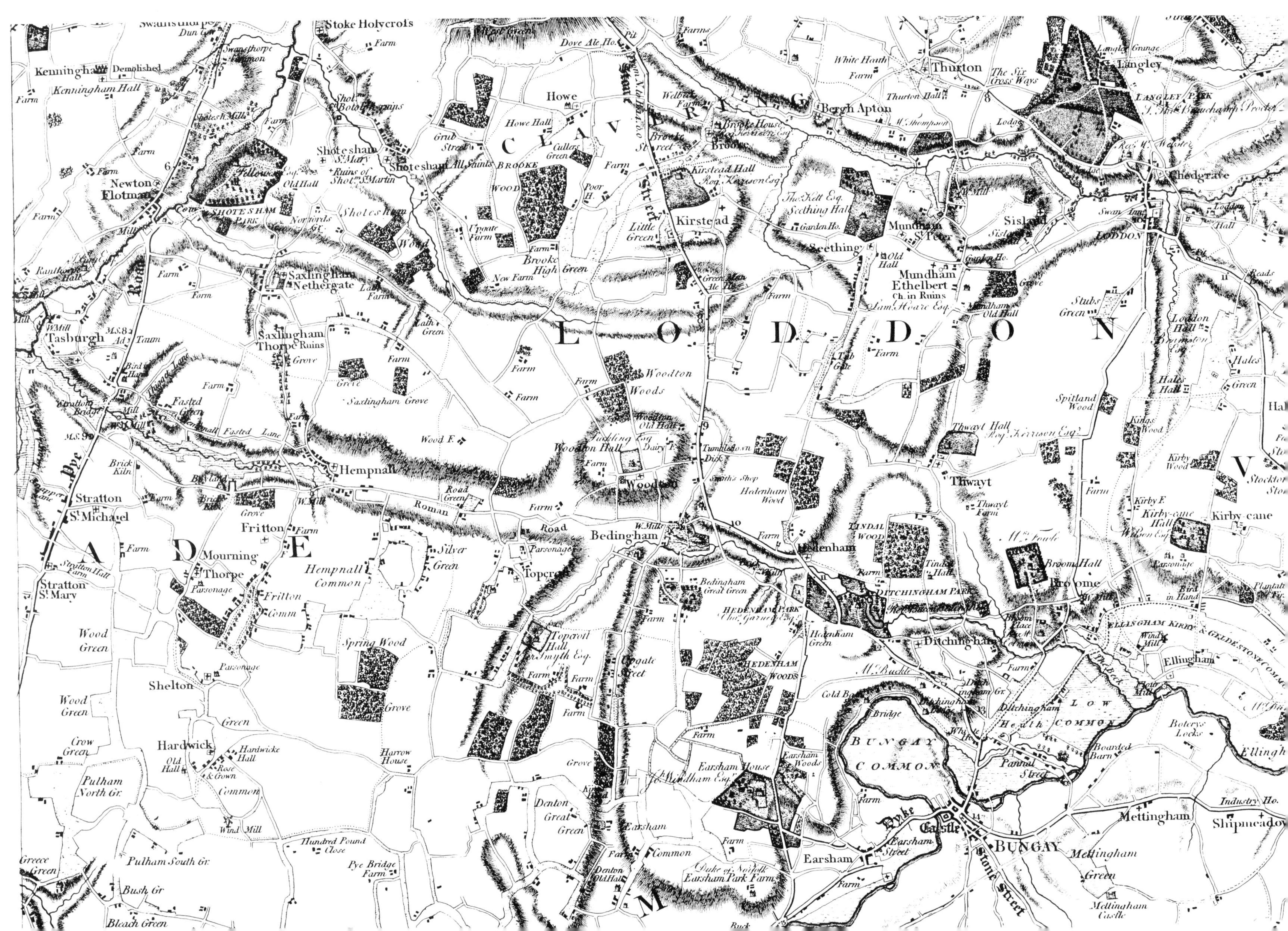

Stoke Holycrofs
Kenningham
Demolished
Kenningham Hall
Shotesham St. Mary
Shotesham All Saints
Newton Flotman
SHOTESHAM PARK
Howe
Howe Hall
CLAVERING
BROOKE WOOD
Brooke High Green
Kirstead Hall
Kirstead
Little Green
Thurton
Thurton Hall
Bergh Apton
The Six Cross Ways
Langley
LANGLEY PARK
Chedgrave
Seething Hall
Seething
Mundham St. Peter
Mundham Ethelbert
Ch. in Ruins
Sisland
LODDON
Loddon Hall
Stubs Green
Saxlingham Nethergate
Saxlingham Thorpe Ruins
Saxlingham Grove
Tasburgh
LODDON
Woodton Woods
Woodton Old Hall
Woodton Hall
Woodton
Hempnall
Fasted Lane
Stratton St. Michael
Fritton
Mourning Thorpe
Hempnall Common
Silver Green
Roman Road
Bedingham
Topcroft
Hedenham
Hedenham Wood
Thwayt Hall
Thwayt
Spitland Wood
Kirby-cane
Kirby-cane Hall
TINDAL WOOD
Broom Hall
Broome
DITCHINGHAM PARK
Ditchingham
Ellingham
Stratton St. Mary
Wood Green
Shelton
Spring Wood
Toperoft Hall
Bedingham Great Green
HEDENHAM PARK
HEDENHAM WOODS
Upgate Street
Hardwick
Hardwicke Hall
Pulham North Gr.
Harrow House
Earsham House
Earsham Woods
BUNGAY COMMON
Low Common
Mettingham
Shipmeadow
Denton Great Green
Earsham
Castle
BUNGAY
Earsham Street
Stone Street
Mettingham Green
Mettingham Castle
Pulham South Gr.
Hundred Pound Close
Pye Bridge Farm
Duke of Norfolk Earsham Park Farm
Bush Gr
Bleach Green
Greece Green

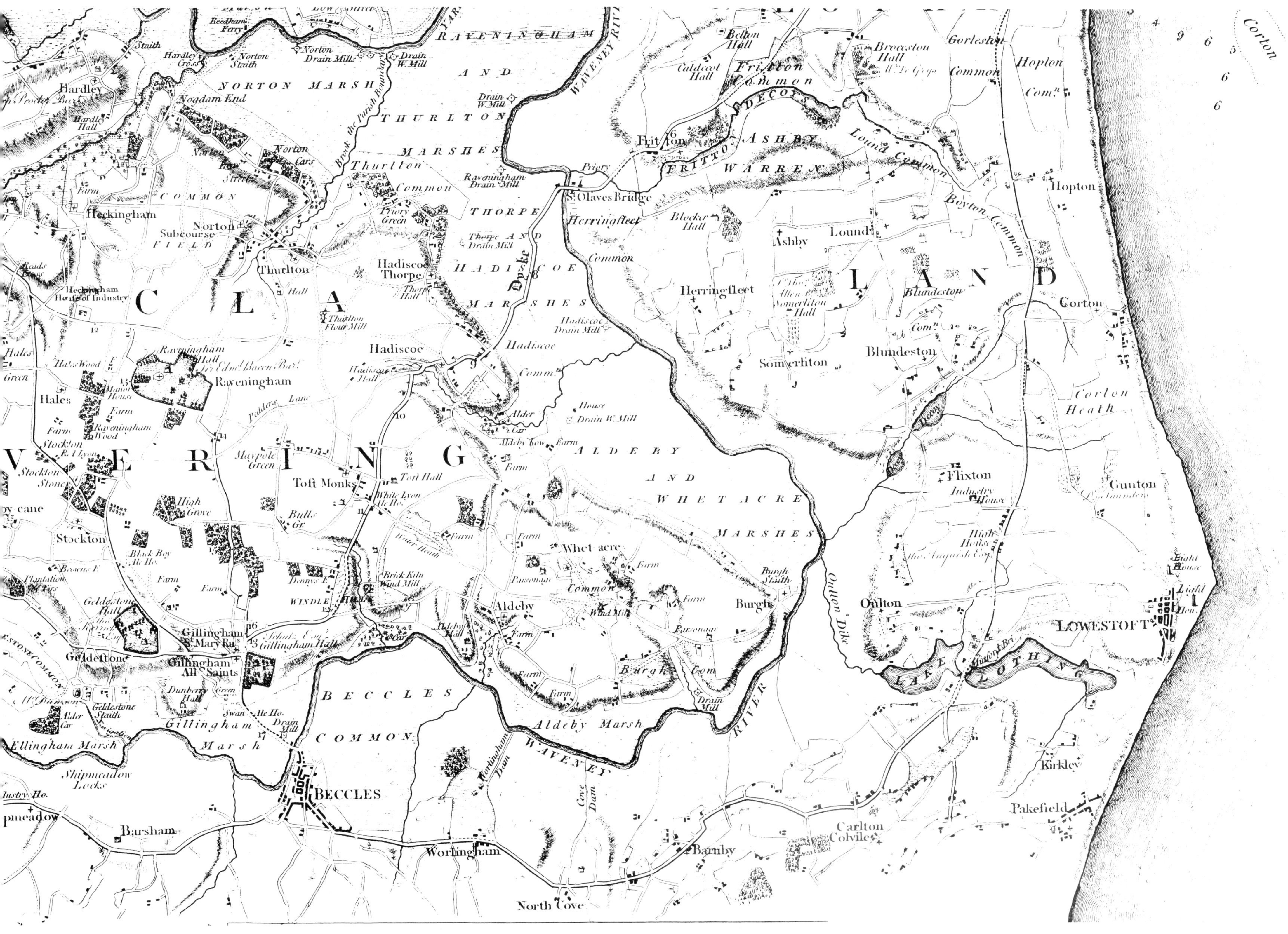

Reedham Ferry
Norton Drain Mills
Drain W. Mill
Hardley Cross
Norton Staith
Hardley
Hardley Hall
Nogdam End
NORTON MARSH
RAVENINGHAM AND THURLTON MARSHES
WAVENEY RIVER
Brook the Parish Boundary
Norton Cars
Thurlton Common
COMMON
Heckingham
Norton
Subcourse
FIELD
Thurlton
Priory Green
THORPE
Thorpe AND Drain Mill
Raveningham Drain Mill
Priory
St. Olaves Bridge
Herringfleet
Common
Belton Hall
Caldecot Hall
Fritton Common
DECOYS
Brocesston Hall
Gorleston Common
Hopton Com.
Fritton
FRITTON ASHBY WARREN
Lound Common
Boyton Common
Hopton
Blocker Hall
Ashby
Lound
Corton
HADISCOE MARSHES
Hadiscoe Thorpe
Thorpe Hall
Dyke
Heckingham House of Industry
C L A
Thurlton Flour Mill
Hadiscoe Drain Mill
Hadiscoe Comm.
Herringfleet
Somerliton Hall
L A N D
Blundeston
Corton
Com.
Hadiscoe
Hadiscoe Hall
Raveningham Hall
Raveningham
Somerliton
Blundeston
Hales
Hales Wood
Green
Manor House
Farm
Raveningham Wood
Padders Lane
Alder Car
House Drain W. Mill
Corton Heath
Decoy
Stockton
V E R I N G
Maypole Green
Toft Monks
Toft Hall
White Lyon Ale Ho.
ALDEBY AND WHET ACRE MARSHES
Flixton
Industry House
Gunton
High Grove
Bulls Gr.
Stockton
Black Boy Ale Ho.
Wash Heath
Whet acre
High House
Light House
Plantation
Geldestone Hall
Brick Kiln Wind Mill
WINDLE HILLS
Farm
Parsonage
Common
Wind Mill
Burgh Staith
Burgh
Oulton Dike
Oulton
Light House
LOWESTOFT
Gillingham St. Mary
Gillingham Hall
Aldeby
Aldeby Hall
Parsonage
Geldestone
Gillingham All Saints
BECCLES COMMON
Burgh Com.
Drain Mill
RIVER
LAKE LOTHING
Mutford Bri.
Dunberry Hall
Geldestone Staith
Swan Ale Ho.
Drain Mill
Gillingham Marsh
Ellingham Marsh
Aldeby Marsh
WAVENEY
Shipmeadow Locks
Worlingham Dam
Cove Dam
Kirkley
BECCLES
Barsham
Worlingham
Barnby
Carlton Colville
Pakefield
North Cove

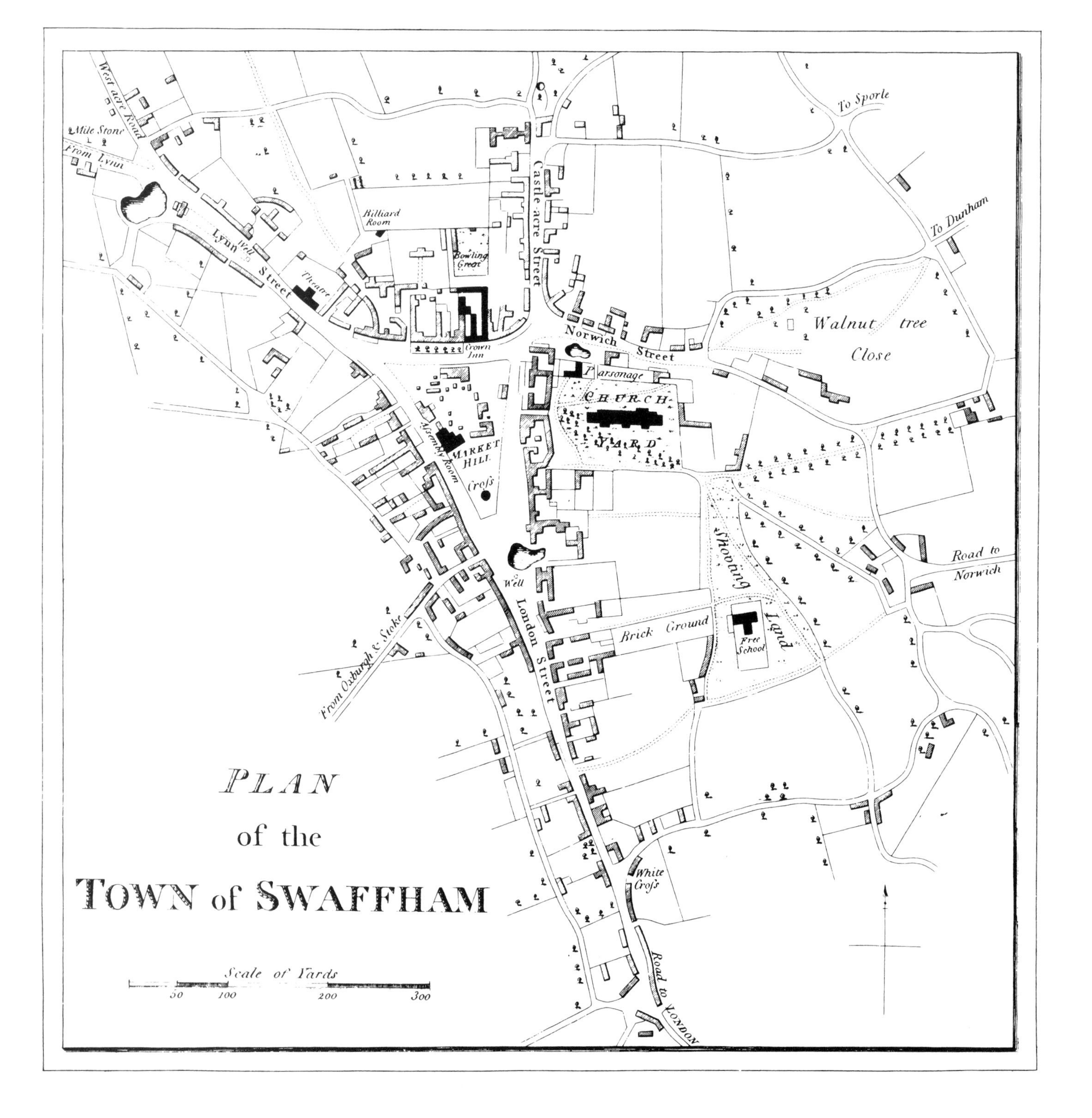
PLAN
of the
TOWN of SWAFFHAM
Scale of Yards
50
100
200
300
West acre Road
Mile Stone
From Lynn
Lynn Street
Well
Theatre
Billiard Room
Bowling Green
Castle acre Street
Crown Inn
Norwich Street
To Sporle
To Dunham
Walnut tree Close
Parsonage
CHURCH YARD
MARKET HILL
Assembly Room
Cross
Well
London Street
From Oxburgh & Stoke
Brick Ground
Shooting Land
Free School
Road to Norwich
White Cross
Road to LONDON

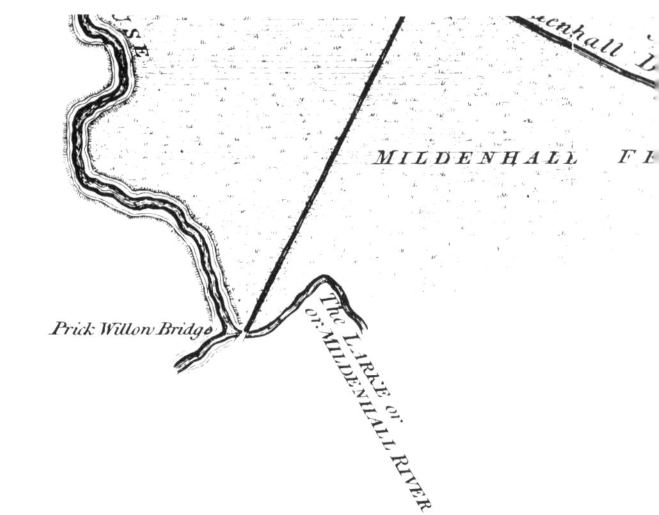
MILDENHALL
Prick Willow Bridge
The LARKE or MILDENHALL RIVER

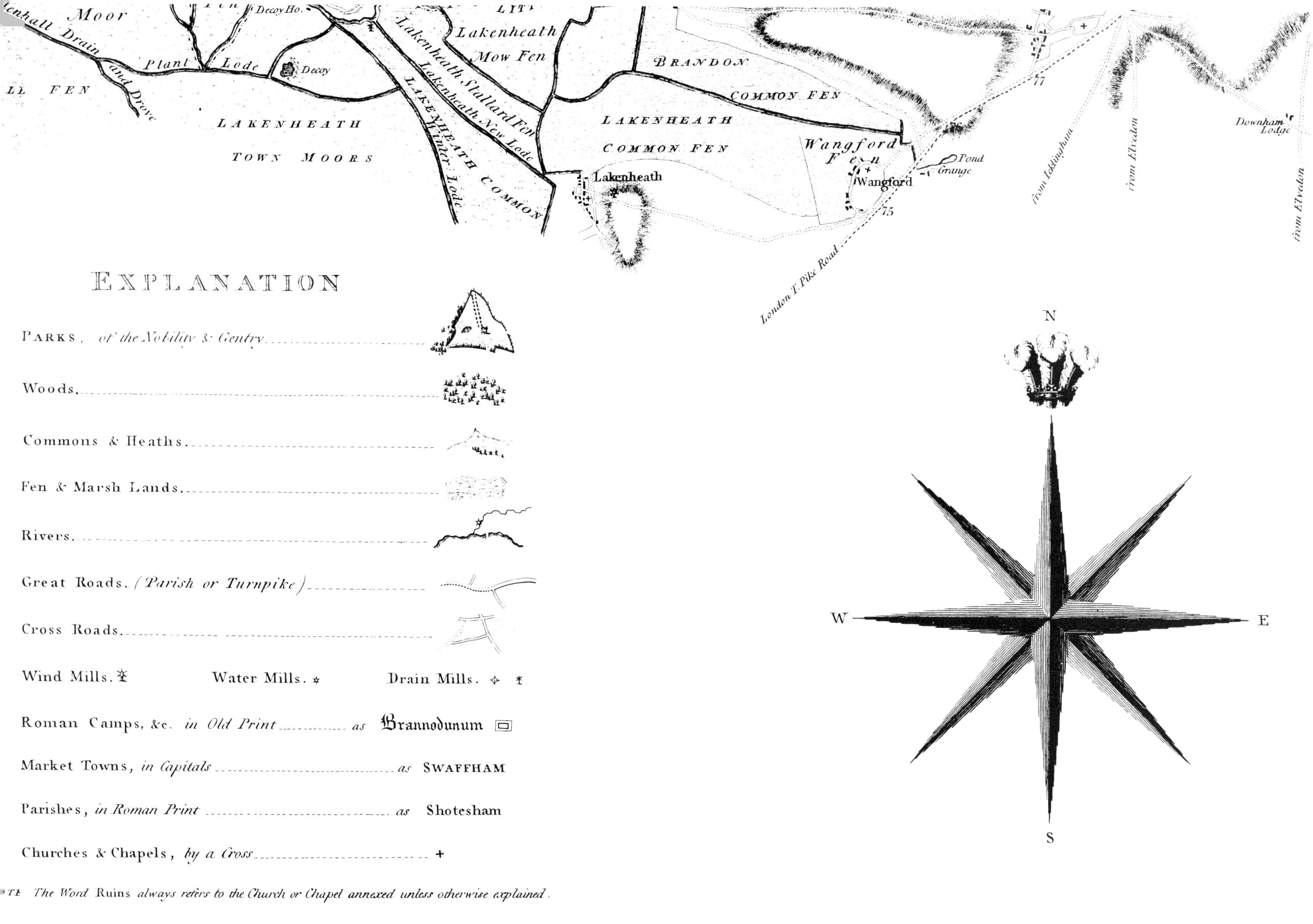
Moor
Decoy Ho.
Lakenheath
Mow Fen
Plant Lode
Decoy
FEN
LAKENHEATH
TOWN MOORS
Lakenheath Stallard Fen
Lakenheath New Lode
LAKENHEATH COMMON
Winter Lode
BRANDON
COMMON FEN
LAKENHEATH
COMMON FEN
Wangford Fen
Lakenheath
Wangford
Pond Grange
Downham Lodge
from Icklingham
from Elvedon
from Elvedon
London T. Pike Road
77
76
75
EXPLANATION
Parks, of the Nobility & Gentry
Woods.
Commons & Heaths.
Fen & Marsh Lands.
Rivers.
Great Roads. (Parish or Turnpike)
Cross Roads.
Wind Mills.
Water Mills.
Drain Mills.
Roman Camps, &c. in Old Print as Brannodunum
Market Towns, in Capitals as SWAFFHAM
Parishes, in Roman Print as Shotesham
Churches & Chapels, by a Cross +
The Word Ruins always refers to the Church or Chapel annexed unless otherwise explained.
N
W
E
S

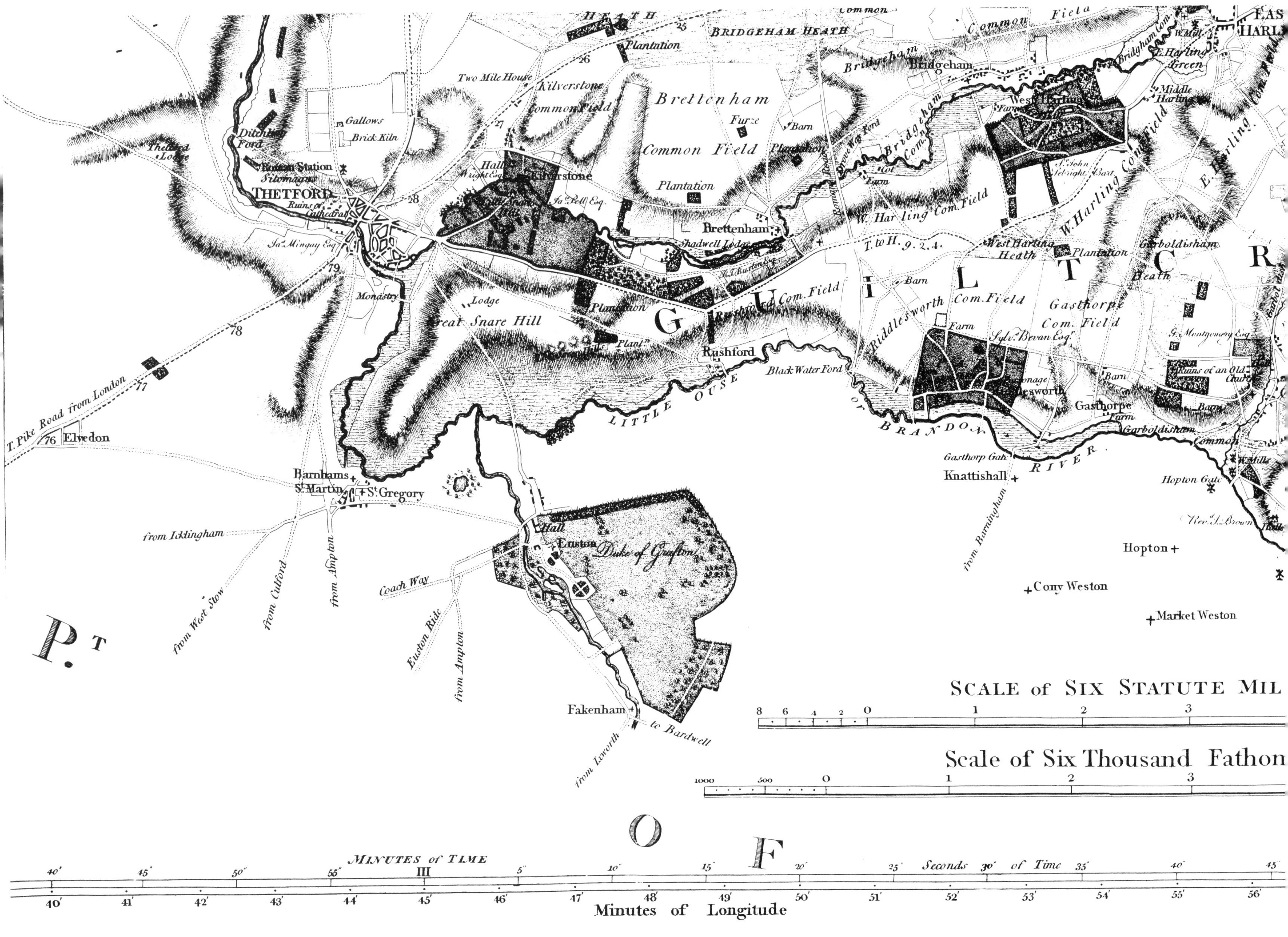

THETFORD
Roman Station Sitomagus
Ruins of Cathedral
Ditchin Ford
Thetford Lodge
Gallows
Brick Kiln
Two Mile House
Kilverstone Common Field
Kilverstone
Brettenham Common Field
Furze
Plantation
BRIDGEHAM HEATH
Bridgeham
Bridgeham Com.
West Harling
Middle Harling
E. Harling Green
S.r John Sebright Bar.t
W. Harling Com. Field
E. Harling Com. Field
Brettenham
Shadwell Lodge
T. to H.
West Harling Heath
Garboldisham Heath
Garboldisham Common
Monastry
Lodge
Great Snare Hill
Rushford Com. Field
Rushford
Black Water Ford
LITTLE OUSE
OR BRANDON RIVER
Riddlesworth Com. Field
Gasthorpe Com. Field
Sylv.r Bevan Esq.r
G. Montgomery Esq.
Ruins of an Old Church
Gasthorpe
Gasthorp Gate
Knattishall
Hopton Gate
Hopton
Cony Weston
Market Weston
G U I L T C R
T. Pike Road from London
Elvedon
Barnhams St. Martin
St. Gregory
from Icklingham
from West Stow
from Culford
from Ampton
Coach Way
Euston Ride
Hall
Euston
Duke of Grafton
Fakenham
to Bardwell
from Ixworth
from Barningham
P. T
O F
SCALE of SIX STATUTE MIL
Scale of Six Thousand Fathon
MINUTES of TIME
Seconds of Time
Minutes of Longitude

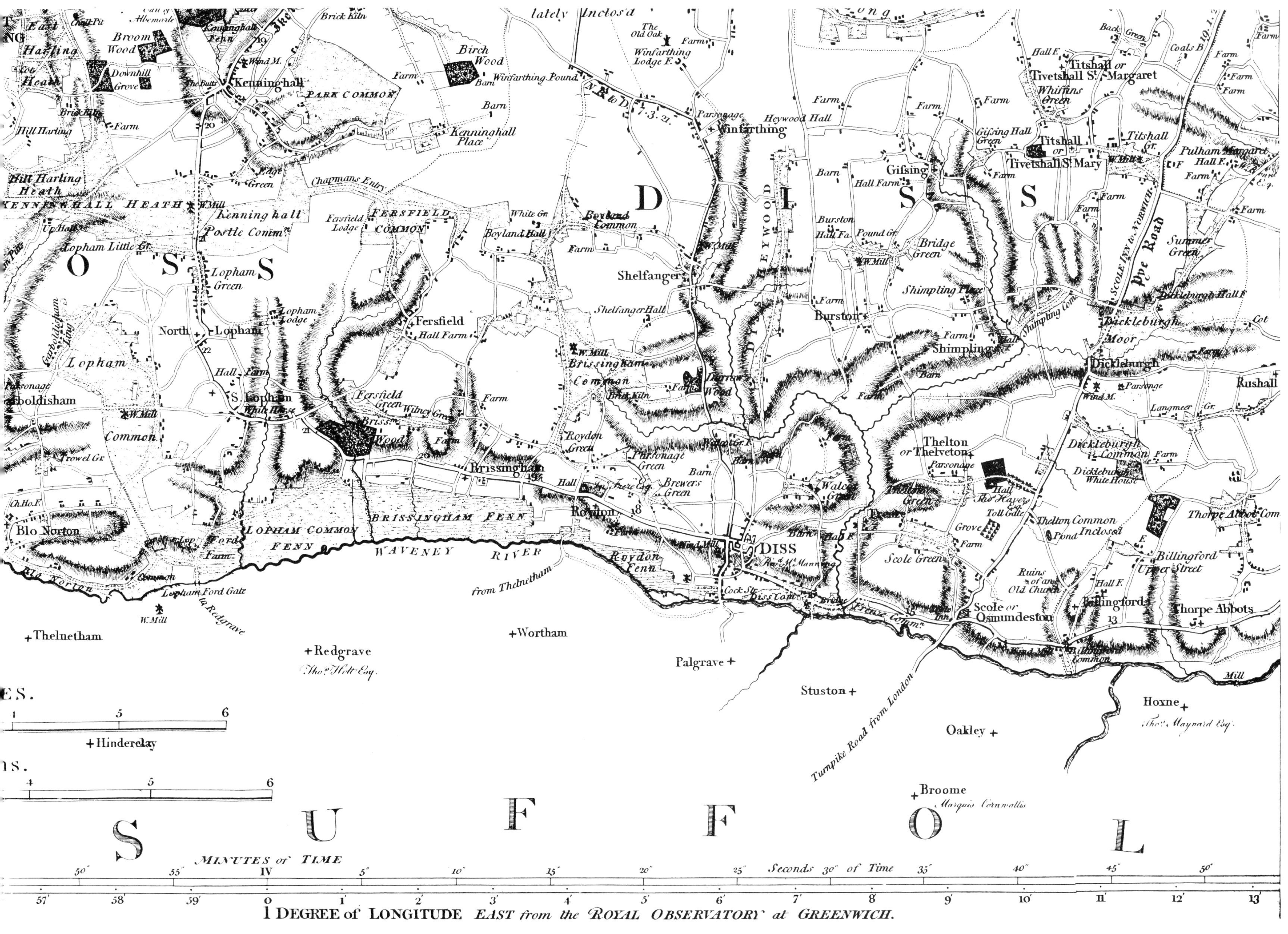

East Harling
Broom Wood
Downhill Grove
Hill Harling
Hill Harling Heath
Kenninghall Heath
Kenninghall
Park Common
Birch Wood
Winfarthing Pound
Kenninghall Place
Chapmans Entry
Kenning hall Postle Common
Fersfield Lodge
Fersfield Common
Boyland Common
Boyland Hall
Lopham Little Gr.
Lopham Green
Lopham Lodge
North Lopham
Lopham
S. Lopham
Garboldisham Ling
Garboldisham
Common
Trowel Gr.
Blo Norton
Lopham Ford Gate
Lopham Common Fenn
Brissingham Fenn
Waveney River
from Thelnetham
Fersfield
Hall Farm
Fersfield Green
Wilney Green
Briss. Wood
Brissingham
Brissingham Common
Roydon Green
Roydon
Roydon Fenn
Parsonage Green
Brewers Green
Frere Esq.
Shelfanger
Shelfanger Hall
Darrow Wood
Heywood
Winfarthing
Winfarthing Lodge F.
The Old Oak
lately Inclos'd
Heywood Hall
Burston
Burston Hall Fa.
Pound Gr.
Bridge Green
Gissing
Gissing Hall Green
Shimpling Place
Shimpling
Shimpling Com.
Titshall or Tivetshall St. Margaret
Whiffins Green
Titshall or Tivetshall St. Mary
Titshall Gr.
Pulham Margaret
Pye Road
Scole Inn to Norwich
Summer Green
Dickleburgh
Dickleburgh Moor
Dickleburgh Common
Dickleburgh White House
Langmeer Gr.
Rushall
Thelton or Thelveton
Thelton Common Inclosed
Toll Gate
The Havers
Walcot Green
Scole Green
Ruins of an Old Church
Scole or Osmundeston
Frenze Comm.
Diss
Revd. Mr. Manning
Cock Str.
Diss Com.
Billingford Upper Street
Billingford
Billingford Common
Thorpe Abbots
Thorpe Abbots Com.
Thelnetham
Redgrave
Thos. Holt Esq.
Wortham
Palgrave
Stuston
Hoxne
Thos. Maynard Esq.
Oakley
Hinderclay
Turnpike Road from London
Broome
Marquis Cornwallis
D I S S
S U F F O L
Minutes of Time
Seconds of Time
1 DEGREE of LONGITUDE EAST from the ROYAL OBSERVATORY at GREENWICH.

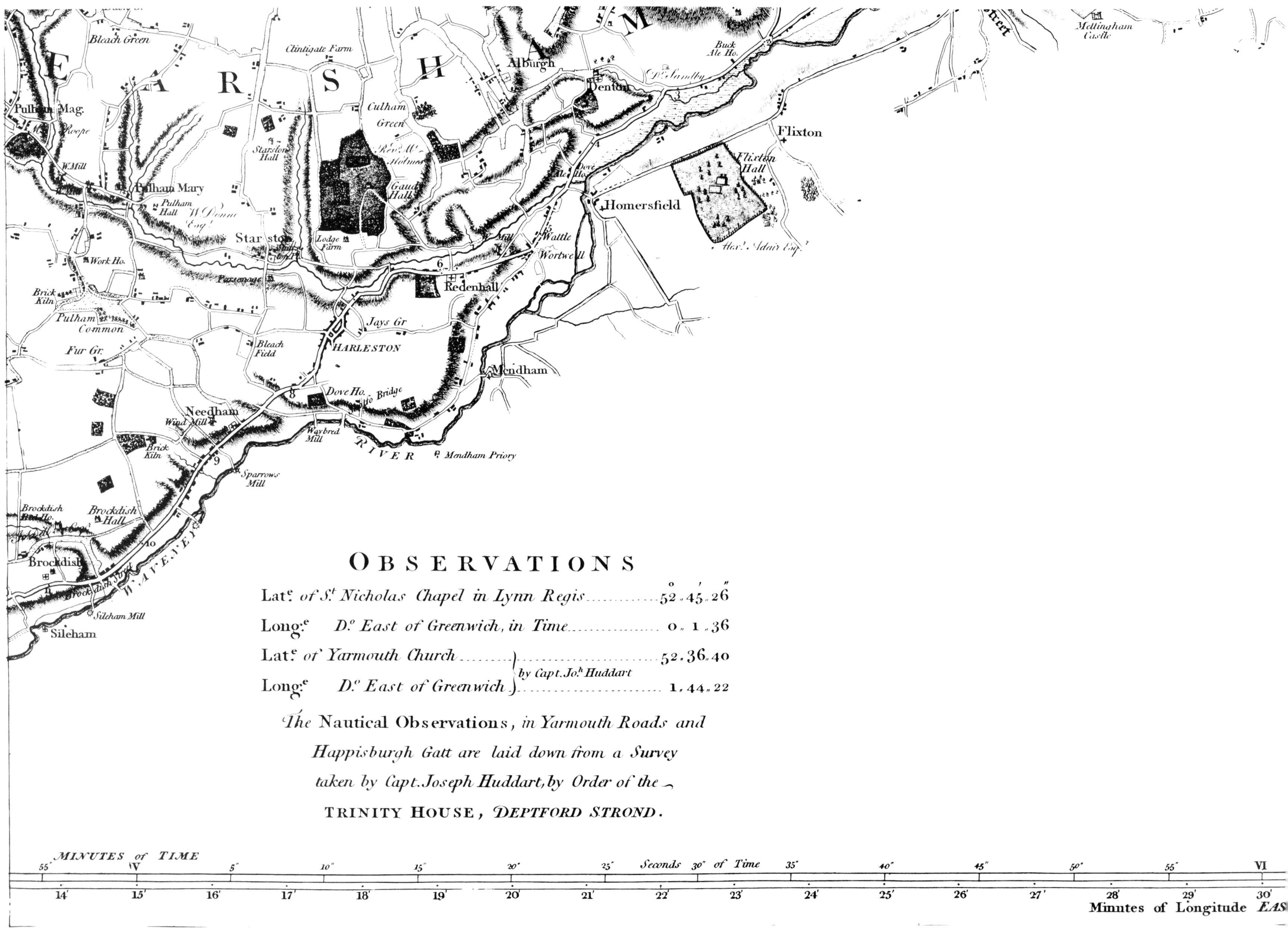
E A R S H A M
Bleach Green
Clintigate Farm
Alburgh
Buck Ale Ho.
Mettingham Castle
Dr. Sandby
Denton
Pulham Mag.
Culham Green
Flixton
Starston Hall
Rev. Mr. Holmes
W.Mill
Pulham Mary
Gaud Hall
Dove Ho.
Flixton Hall
Pulham Hall
W. Donne Esq.
Homersfield
Starston
Lodge Farm
Wattle
Alexr. Adair Esq.
Work Ho.
Wortwell
Parsonage
Redenhall
Brick Kiln
Pulham Common
Jays Gr
Fur Gr.
Bleach Field
HARLESTON
Mendham
Dove Ho.
Bridge
Needham
Wind Mill
Waybred Mill
Brick Kiln
RIVER
Mendham Priory
Sparrows Mill
Brockdish Hall
Brockdish Hall
Brockdish
WAVENEY
Silcham Mill
Sileham
OBSERVATIONS
Latᵉ. of Sᵗ. Nicholas Chapel in Lynn Regis .... 52° 45′ 26″
Longᵉ. Dᵒ. East of Greenwich, in Time 0. 1. 36
Latᵉ. of Yarmouth Church 52. 36. 40
Longᵉ. Dᵒ. East of Greenwich 1. 44. 22
by Capt. Joʰ. Huddart
The Nautical Observations, in Yarmouth Roads and
Happisburgh Gatt are laid down from a Survey
taken by Capt. Joseph Huddart, by Order of the
TRINITY HOUSE, DEPTFORD STROND.
MINUTES of TIME
55″
V
5″
10″
15″
20″
25″
Seconds 30″ of Time
35″
40″
45″
50″
55″
VI
14′
15′
16′
17′
18′
19′
20′
21′
22′
23′
24′
25′
26′
27′
28′
29′
30′
Minutes of Longitude EAS

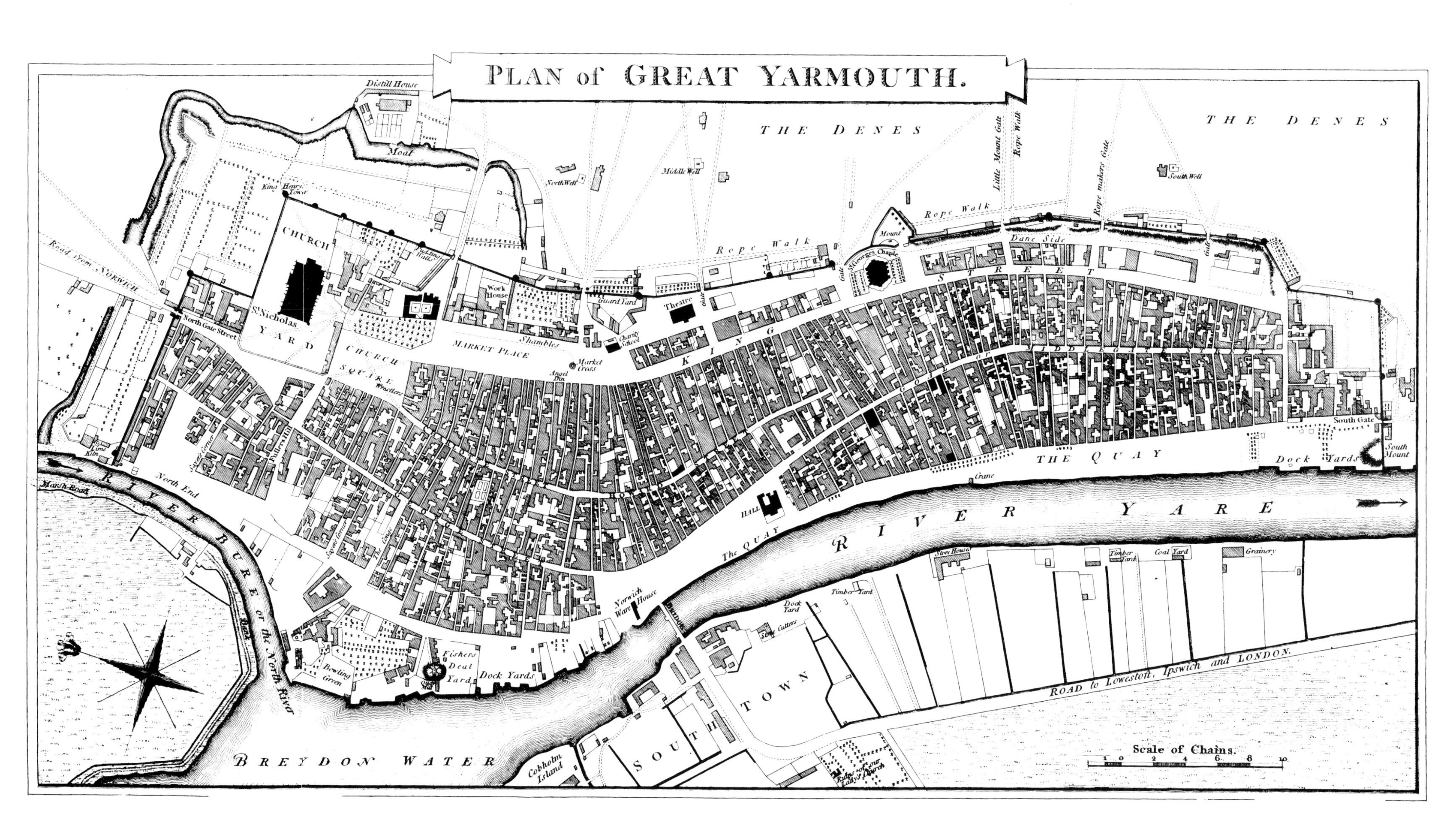
PLAN of GREAT YARMOUTH.
THE DENES
THE DENES
Distill House
Moat
King Henry's Tower
CHURCH
St. Nicholas
YARD
CHURCH
SQUARE
North Gate Street
MARKET PLACE
Market Cross
Shambles
Work House
Guard Yard
Theatre
Charity School
Rope Walk
Rope Walk
Mount
St. Georges Chaple
Little Mount Gate
Rope Walk
Rope makers Gate
North Well
Middle Well
South Well
Dane Side
KING
STREET
South Gate
South Mount
THE QUAY
Dock Yards
Crane
RIVER YARE
HALL
The QUAY
Norwich Ware House
Road from NORWICH
Lime Kiln
Marsh Road
RIVER BURE or the North River
North End
BREYDON WATER
Bowling Green
Fishers Deal Yard
Dock Yards
Dock Yard
Timber Yard
Store House
Timber Yard
Coal Yard
Grainery
Cobholm Island
SOUTH TOWN
SOUTH TOWN
ROAD to Lowestoft, Ipswich and LONDON.
Scale of Chains.
1 0 2 4 6 8 10